Living by Grace

Pauline Webb is a broadcaster, writer and lay preacher. A former Vice-Moderator of the World Council of Churches and Vice-President of the Methodist Church, she has wide ecumenical experience which is reflected both in her writings and in her campaigning commitment to global justice and peace. Her autobiography, *World Wide Webb*, was published by Canterbury Press in 2006.

Nadir Dinshaw was born in one of Karachi's leading Parsee families and converted to Christianity in the 1960s. His gift for friendship and his generosity were legendary. He died in 2002. The Archbishop of Canterbury preached at his memorial service.

Living by Grace

Moments of grace for every day of the year

Compiled by
Pauline Webb
and
Nadir Dinshaw

CANTERBURY
PRESS
Norwich

in association with
CAIRNS PUBLICATIONS

British Library Cataloguing in Publication data

A catalogue record for this book is available
from the British Library

978 1 85311 849 4

First published in 2001 by Cairns Publications,
Dwylan, Stryd Fawr, Harlech, Gwynedd LL46 2YA

This edition published jointly by Canterbury Press
and Cairns Publications

www.cottercairns.co.uk
www.canterburypress.co.uk

Printed in Great Britain by
William Clowes Ltd, Beccles, Suffolk

CONTENTS

Dedicated to the memory of
Nadir Dinshaw

FOREWORD

Grace is the reunion of life with life, the reconciliation of the self with itself. Grace is the acceptance of that which is rejected. Grace transforms fate into a meaningful destiny; it charges guilt into confidence and courage. There is something triumphant in the word "grace": in spite of the abounding of sin, grace abounds much more.

These famous words by Paul Tillich are placed as the second entry in this anthology, and they make a fitting epigraph to a lovely book. When the words were first published in *The Shaking of the Foundations* the world was not aware of the personal anguish that lay behind them. Tillich struggled all his life with the compulsions of sexuality, and we can hear echoes of that unresolved struggle in the passage just quoted. It goes on: "Grace strikes us when we are in great pain and restlessness . . . It strikes us when our disgust for our own being, our indifference, our weakness, our hostility, and our lack of direction and composure have become intolerable for us. It strikes us when year after year the longed for perfection of life does not appear, when the old compulsions reign within us as they have for decades, when despair destroys all joy and courage." Then there follow the words that have been uttered from so many pulpits, whispered in so many confessionals, and fastened upon by so many unhappy souls: "It is as though a voice were saying: 'You are accepted. You are accepted, accepted by that which is greater than you, and the name of which you do not know . . . Simply accept that fact that you are accepted.' If that happens to us, we experience grace."

There is no attempt by Tillich to define grace here, to offer some kind of theological account of it or locate it in some kind of justifying context. Instead, he reminds us of the sheer experience of grace and the way it comes flooding in, often when we least expect it, from surprising people and strange places.

In my experience, one of the most potent mediators of grace is
the written word. I can trudge through reams of text and suddenly
hit upon a moment of grace that calls to something in me, some
need for assurance or acceptance, and reminds me that, in spite of
all I know against myself, I am held in the unconditional love of
God. That is why, over the years, like Pauline Webb and Nadir
Dinshaw, I have kept what used to be called 'a commonplace
book', a trove of treasures brought back from years of wandering
through the writings and remembrances of fascinating people,
some unknown and some well known. As well as maintaining my
own anthologies, I have devoured the anthologies of others and
have about thirty of them in my own library.

Many people sneer at the use of anthologies, much in the way
they sneer at Classic FM, because, it is alleged, they take the pain
and tedium out of cherry picking and give you the best fruit
without asking any effort from you. The puritan in me responds to
this criticism with a certain discomfort. It is true that we would
never have had the sudden moments of illumination and grace if
the writer or composer had not struggled through the long periods
of argument and research. But the fact remains that the moments
of sudden brilliance and clarity can usually stand on their own,
even if they are better understood within the total context of their
creation. And who would begrudge busy people, who cannot find
the time for their own explorations, the joy of hearing about other
people's discoveries? I see no reason, therefore, why we cannot
affirm the value of both exercises. In any case, one can easily lead
back into the other. Indeed, when I read the quotation from *The
Shaking of the Foundations,* not only was I delighted to be reminded
of it, but also it made me determined to go back to the original
sermon from which it came and read the whole of it again.

Pauline Webb and Nadir Dinshaw are born anthologists. They
have read the texts from which they draw: they have dug deep in
the fields that contain the hidden treasures. Like others who have
published anthologies they want to share their discoveries with
others. In the case of these two compilers, however, something else

is going on. Pauline and Nadir are lovers of humanity. The pastoral instinct in them, the drive to help others, is strongly developed. *Living by Grace* is much more than a way of sharing their delight in the examples of human wisdom and beauty that they have collected over the years: it is an act of ministry, a work of service. That is why I am convinced that this book about Grace will mediate Grace to others. And that is the highest gift any human being can offer another.

RICHARD HOLLOWAY
formerly Bishop of Edinburgh
in the Scottish Episcopal Church
Edinburgh, January 2001

PREFACE
to the second edition

One of the compensations of growing older is that one has more time to enjoy old treasures stored up in cupboards where they have lain forgotten for a long time. Among my treasures is a commonplace book in which over the years I have jotted down quotations culled from a variety of sources. They make a haphazard collection, and I have been far too inefficient in noting down where they came from or the occasion which brought them to my notice. But now in my old age, each extract recalls some experience which I have found echoed in a book or an article. The words I scribbled down in the course of a busy life I can now savour at my leisure.

An even greater compensation of old age is the time to be with friends. Someone has described friends as 'the family we choose for ourselves'. But friends have brought such blessing into my life that I can only believe that they have come as God's gift to me. Certainly the meeting between Nadir Dinshaw and myself was providential. We came from such different backgrounds that it seems like a miracle that our paths ever crossed. The fact that we met many years ago after a service in St Paul's Cathedral in London, in the home of that great prophet for justice and peace, John Collins, would seem to suggest indeed that the hand of God was in our coming together. The theme of the service had been racial justice, and immediately we recognized in each other committed allies in the struggle – Nadir, who himself came from Pakistan, was a tireless and generous supporter of the Joint Campaign for the Welfare of Immigrants, and I at that time was fully involved in the World Council of Churches' Programme to Combat Racism.

Our friendship grew and became one in which we shared not only our concerns about public issues but also our more personal pilgrimage. An avid reader himself, Nadir most generously introduced me to many treasures of spiritual wisdom. It was no surprise to me to find that he too kept a commonplace book. One of our great joys was to share with one another the quotations we had collected over the years.

When he suggested that we should compile an anthology out of our joint collections, the theme that came to my mind was Grace. Nadir himself was a person full of grace. Sadly, since the first edition of this anthology Nadir has reached the end of his earthly pilgrimage, but the memory of his friendship lives on for all of us who were privileged to know him personally and for many more who were influenced and helped by his gracious generosity. In his name I offer this anthology to all who read it with the prayer that you too may find in it words of grace which will enrich your life as they did Nadir's and mine.

PAULINE WEBB
London, August 2007

January

The Meaning of Grace

1 January

Today let candles shed their radiant greeting:
Lo! on our darkness are they not Thy light
Leading us, haply, to our longed-for meeting?
Thou canst illumine even our darkest night.

While all the powers of Good aid and attend us
Boldly we'll face the future, be it what.it may.
At even and at morn, God will befriend us,
And oh, most surely on each new year's day!

DIETRICH BONHOEFFER

2 January

Grace is the reunion of life with life, the reconciliation of the self with itself. Grace is the acceptance of that which is rejected. Grace transforms fate into a meaningful destiny; it changes guilt into confidence and courage. There is something triumphant in the word 'grace': in spite of the abounding of sin, grace abounds much more.

Grace strikes us when we are in great pain and restlessness. It strikes us when we walk through the dark valley of a meaningless and empty life. It strikes us when we feel our separation is deeper than usual, because we have violated another life, a life which we loved, or from which we were estranged. It strikes us when our disgust for our own being, our indifference, our weakness, our hostility, and our lack of direction and composure have become intolerable for us. It strikes us when year after year the longed for perfection of life does not appear, when the old compulsions reign within us as they have for decades, when despair destroys all joy and courage.

Sometimes at that moment a wave of life breaks into our darkness, and it is as though a voice were saying: "You are accepted. *You are accepted*, accepted by that which is greater than you, and the name of which you do not know. Do not ask for the name now; perhaps you will find it later. Do not try to do anything now; perhaps you will do much. Do not seek for anything; do not perform anything; do not intend anything. *Simply accept that fact that you are accepted.*" If that happens to us, we experience grace.

PAUL TILLICH

3 January

Grace is defined by the dictionary as attractiveness, ease and refinement of manners, unconstrained goodwill, divine regeneration and inspired influence. For me, grace is the dynamic flowering of God's love. When theologians describe grace in all its forms, they speak of a love so abundant, so selfless, so endlessly overflowing, that it surpasses description.

STANISLAUS KENNEDY

4 January

Grace is the opposite of Disgrace.

A boy called Jimmy Price one day came into the workshop of Edison, the inventor. What did he want? He wanted to be an inventor. Where was he going to live? In the workshop. It was better than where he had been living anyway. Where was he going to sleep? He would be all right under one of the big benches. Remembering his own start in life, Edison began by sending him for a meal.

More than nine thousand attempts had been made in that workshop to invent an electric light, and all had failed. One more try was made, using a carbon filament in place of metal. It was a day's work for three or four men, the glass blower, the metal workers, and the electrician. When the bulb was ready, the proto-type of electric bulbs soon to be seen all over the world, they called Jimmy to take it up to Edison. "And be careful," they said.

He was careful – at first. He began slowly, then hurried,

tripped, and fell. The bulb was broken, and there was nothing else to do but to begin all over again to make another. When that was ready, Edison himself called for Jimmy to bring it up to his room. The boy, who was still weeping behind a door, came out, and Edison make him carry the bulb upstairs.

"There's one thing about mistakes, Jimmy." he said. "They need not be permanent."

ALLEN BIRTWHISTLE

5 January

The ignorant need to be instructed, not punished. You do not strike a blind man, you take him by the hand to lead him.

DIONYSIUS THE AREOPAGITE

6 January

By Twelfth Night Helena rallied and on the eve set out by litter along the five rough miles to the shrine of the Nativity...The low vault was full of lamps and the air close and still. Silver bells announced the coming of the three, vested, bearded monks, who, like the kings of old, prostrated themselves before the altar. So the long liturgy began.

Helena knew little Greek and her thoughts were not in the words nor anywhere in the immediate scene. She forgot even her quest and was dead to everything except the swaddled child long ago and those three royal sages who had come from so far to adore him.

"This is my day," she thought, "and these are my kind."

"Like me," she said to them, "you were late in coming. The shepherds were here long before, even the cattle. They had joined the chorus of angels before you were on your way. For you the primordial discipline of the heavens was relaxed and a new defiant light blazed amid the disconcerted stars.

"Yet you came, and were not turned away. You too found

room before the manger. Your gifts were not needed, but they were accepted and put carefully by, for they were brought with love. In that new order of charity that had just come to life, there was room for you too. You were not lower in the eyes of the holy family than the ox or the ass.

"You are my especial patrons," said Helena, "and patrons of all late-comers, of all who have a tedious journey to make to the truth, of all who are confused with knowledge and speculation, of all who through politeness make themselves partners in guilt, of all who stand in danger by reason of their talents.

"Dear cousins, pray for me," said Helena, "and for my poor overloaded son. May he, too, before the end find kneeling space in the straw. Pray for the great, lest they perish utterly...For His sake who did not reject your curious gifts, pray always for all the learned, the oblique, the delicate. Let them not be quite forgotten at the Throne of God when the simple come into their kingdom."

EVELYN WAUGH

7 January

Why were infants so important for the new era? Children had never been so much in evidence. Now for the first time an infant became a symbolic figure and His Mother with Him. Mother and Child...There we have a child who seems to be not in the past but still ahead of us in future prospect. The germ not of history but of eternity, and through the birth of His Mother a constant reminder that in God the Child is never extinct.

ABRAM TERTS

8 January

To Daniel, my new-born son:

Looking at your sleeping face, inches away from mine, listening to your occasional sigh and gurgle, I wonder how I could ever have thought glory and prizes and praise were sweeter than life. And it's also true that I am pained, perhaps haunted is a better word, by the memory suddenly so vivid now, of each suffering child I have come across on my journeys.

FERGAL KEANE

9 January

I remember something I was told when I was a very small boy...In the larder there was a stack of apples. A small boy wanted an apple. He had been told by some grown-up that he must not take things from the larder without permission...Why not take one? Nobody would know. It just seemed common sense. Nobody would see him. Was that true? Nobody? One person would. That was God. He sees everything you do, and then punishes you for the wrongdoing, so I was told.

It took me many, many years to recover from that story. Deep in my subconscious was the idea of God as somebody who was always watching us just to see if we were doing anything wrong. He was an authority figure, like a teacher or a policeman or even a bishop.

Now, many years later, I have an idea that God would have said to the small boy, "Take two ..."

BASIL HUME

10 January

Know you what it is to be a child? It is to have a spirit yet stream-
ing from the waters of baptism; it is to believe in love, to believe
in loveliness, to believe in belief. It is to be so little that the elves
can reach to whisper in your ear; it is to turn pumpkins into
coaches and mice into horses, lowliness into loftiness, and nothing into everything; for each child has its fairy godmother in each
soul. It is to live in a nutshell and to count yourself the King of
infinite space; it is to know not as yet that you are under sentence
of life, nor petition that it be commuted into death.

When we become conscious in dreaming that we dream, the
dream is on the point of breaking. When we become conscious
in living that we live, the ill dream is but first beginning.

FRANCIS THOMPSON

11 January

Live slowly, think slowly, for time is a mystery.

Never forget that love requires always that you be the greatest
person you are capable of being.

Be grateful for the manifold dreams of creation and the many
ways of the unnumbered peoples.

Be grateful for life as you live it, and may a wonderful light
always guide you on the unfolding road.

BEN OKRI

12 January

God's love for us is not the reason why we should love Him. God's
love for us is the reason for us to love ourselves. How could we
love ourselves without this motive?...To love a stranger as oneself
implies the reverse...to love oneself as a stranger.

SIMONE WEIL

13 January

God continually and earnestly offers Himself as a God of grace, and urges even those who spurn Him and are His enemies to accept Him as such...This is grace: the forgiveness of sins for the sake of the Lord Jesus Christ, the covering up of all sins. Grace makes the Law dear to us. And then, sin is no longer there and the Law is no longer against us, but with us.

All the many countless blessings which God gives us here on earth are merely those gifts which last for a time; but His grace and loving regard are the inheritance which endures throughout eternity.

MARTIN LUTHER

14 January

One of the gifts of God I am most grateful for is having met at the age of sixteen a Franciscan priest. I was not yet a Catholic, but a Zoroastrian who was gradually falling in love with Jesus. This Franciscan came into my life at a crucial moment and taught me one solid doctrine – to trust in God by living one day at a time...What other way of life can bring one more peace and certitude of God's love for us? This way of believing in His love, and truly trying to live one day at a time has brought me nothing but blessings and peace. Anxiety about the morrow has never been a headache for me. I have also tried to help others to live like that: sure of God's love for one, and one day at a time. If you've never tried this, please do. You'll find it a great blessing and a peaceful way of living.

MATAJI VANDANA

15 January

God wastes nothing – not even sin. The soul that has struggled and come through is enriched by its experiences, and grace does not merely blot out the evil past but in the most literal sense 'makes it good'.

DOROTHY SAYERS

16 January

Nobody's life flows on such an even course that it does not sometimes come up against a dam and whirl round and round, or somebody throws a stone into the clear water. Something happens to everyone – and he or she must take care that the water stays clear and that heaven and earth are reflected in it.

FRITZ REUTER

17 January

The greatness of our God lies in the fact that He is both tough-minded and tender-hearted. He has qualities both of austerity and of gentleness. The Bible, always clear in stressing both the attributes of God, expresses His tough-mindedness in His justice and wrath and His tender-heartedness in His love and grace. God has two outstretched arms. One is strong enough to surround us with justice, and one is gentle enough to embrace us with grace. On the one hand, God is the God of justice who punished Israel for her wayward deeds; on the other hand He is a forgiving father whose heart was filled with unutterable joy when the prodigal returned home.

MARTIN LUTHER KING

18 January

There is in operation in the political field a creative factor which does not spring naturally out of man's make-up or even from his economic arrangements and political programmes – a factor that I can only describe as the operation of the grace of God.

It unsnarls logjams, spans unbridgeable gulfs, and resolves apparent deadlocks. I have seen this happen too often in concrete political situations ever to believe that talk about the grace of God is pious cant. It operates through men of affairs who make surprising renunciations and unpredictable sacrifices; who have unaccountable changes of mind and of heart, and as a consequence the stalemate of eyeball-to-eyeball diplomacy is broken and mankind gets on the move again.

COLIN MORRIS

19 January

The last six years afforded me much time and food for thought. I came to the conclusion that the human race is not divided into two opposing camps of good and evil. It is made up of those who are capable of learning and those who are incapable of doing so. Here I am not talking in the narrow sense of acquiring an academic education, but of learning as the process of absorbing those lessons of life that enable us to increase peace and happiness in the world.

AUNG SAN SUU KYI

20 January

God does not love you because you are loveable. You are loveable because God loves you.

DESMOND TUTU

21 January

When do tears come for the alternative believer? They begin to flow at the moment when we see the contradiction between what we hope for and what we really are, when we see the deep gulf between the Love that calls us, and our response to it.

ALAN JONES

22 January

Don't waste life in doubts and fears. Spend yourself on the work before you, well assured that the right performance of this hour's duties will be the best preparation for the hours or ages that follow it.

RALPH WALDO EMERSON

23 January

Mother Teresa used to tell a story of a lonely old man she visited in Melbourne, Australia. "I saw his room in a terrible state, and I wanted to clean his house, his room, and he kept on saying, 'I'm all right.' But I repeated the same words, 'You would be more all right if you would allow me to clean your place.' In the end he allowed me to do so. And there in the room was a beautiful lamp covered with the dirt of many years, and I asked him, 'Why do you not light your lamp?' Then I asked him, 'Will you light the lamp if the Sisters come to see you?' He said, 'Yes, if I hear a human voice I will do it.' And the other day he sent me word, 'Tell my friend the light she lit in my life is still burning.'"

MOTHER TERESA

24 January

The very God! Think, Abib, dost thou think?
So the All-Great were the All-Loving too.
So through the thunder comes a human voice
Saying, "O heart I made, a heart beats here!
Face my hands fashioned see it in myself:
Thou hast no power nor may'st conceive of mine
But love I gave thee with myself to love
And thou must love me who have died for thee."
The madman saith he said so; it is strange.

ROBERT BROWNING

25 January

I am the least of the apostles, unfit to be called an apostle because
I persecuted the church of God. But by the grace of God I am
what I am, and His grace towards me has not been in vain. On
the contrary I worked harder than any of them – though it was
not I, but the grace of God that was in me.

PAUL

26 January

There is a second century description of the apostle in the pages
of the apocryphal *Acts of Paul*: "Small of stature, balding, bow
legs, large eyes, eyebrows meeting, nose slightly hooked – yet his
appearance was full of grace: sometimes he looked more like an
angel than a man." This strange mixture – of a physically
unimpressive man who was yet singularly impressive – fits the
picture given by Chrysostom too who refers to him as "five feet
high, but with a reach beyond the stars".

HUBERT RICHARDS

27 January

After all, life for all its agonies of despair and loss and guilt is exciting and beautiful, amusing and artful and endearing, full of liking and of love, at times a poem and a high adventure, at times noble and at times very gay; and whatever (if anything) is to come after it, we shall not have this life again.

ROSE MACAULAY

28 January

Come, come whoever you are,
Wanderer, worshipper, lover of learning.
It doesn't matter.
Ours is not a caravan of despair.
Come, even if you have broken your vows a thousand times,
Come, come yet again, come.

RUMI

29 January

Our being spreads out far beyond us, and mingles with the beings of others. We live in other people's thoughts, their plans, their dreams...we have an infinite responsibility.

IRIS MURDOCH

30 January

It is easy to speak of people as pointers to God...but most of the time they hide behind a social mask until something happens to make them drop it for a moment or two: the death of a friend, a failure, or a fear realized, the birth of a child or the blossoming of an unexpected love...[H]aving once been given a glimpse of one dull person transformed, it is easier to see the truth of other people hidden behind their opaque protective masks and mimes.

Such glimpses come the way of a clergyman more often perhaps than they do to many other people. It is this which makes it easy every now and again to see the dull ranks of church people become filled with mini Mother Teresas in shabby pews and dowdy hats, and pocket Wesleys and Wilberforces in tired, dilapidated cassocks. To adopt a different metaphor, rather as a medieval stained glass looks grey and lifeless when viewed from outside a church building but from inside lights up in a great richness of colour and splendour of light when the sun comes out, the community of the Church is transformed from time to time when viewed from inside, as the grace of God comes out and illuminates it.

ANTONY BRIDGE

31 January

'The Kingdom'

It's a long way off but inside it
There are quite different things going on:
Festivals at which the poor man
Is king and the consumptive is
Healed: mirrors in which the blind look
At themselves and love looks at them
Back; and industry is for mending
The bent bones and the minds fractured
By life. It's a long way off, but to get
There takes no time and admission
Is free. If you will purge yourself
Of desire and present yourself with
Your need only and the simple offering
Of your faith, green as a leaf.

R. S. THOMAS

February

Moments of Grace

1 February

I count the moments of my mercies up,
I make a list of love and find it full.
I do all this before I sleep.

Others examine consciences. I tell
My beads of gracious moments shining still.
I count my good hours and they guide me well

Into a sleepless night. It's when I fill
Pages with what I think I am made for,
A life of writing poems. Then may they heal

The pain of silence for all those who stare
At stars as I do but are helpless to
Make the bright necklace. May I set ajar

The doors of closed minds. Words come and words go
And poetry is pain as well as passion.
But in the large flights of imagination

I see for one crammed second order so
Explicit that I need no more persuasion.

ELIZABETH JENNINGS

2 February

(Our Lord's) human qualities and character were formed and
influenced by His Mother's virtues...Mary's function in the
Incarnation was not completed when Jesus was born. It was a
continuous task, involving the human formation of the young
man as he grew up from infancy to childhood, and from
childhood to adulthood.

EDWARD SCHILLEBEECKX

3 February

As I write these last words, my thoughts return to you who were my comrades, the stubborn and indomitable peasants of Nepal. Once more I hear the laughter with which you greeted every hardship. Once more I see you in your bivouacs or about your fires, on forced march or in the trenches, now shivering with wet and cold, now scorched by a pitiless and burning sun. Uncomplaining you endure hunger and thirst and wounds, and at the last your unwavering lines disappear into the smoke and wrath of battle. Bravest of the brave, most generous of the generous, never had country more faithful friends than you.

RALPH TURNER

4 February

Open your window, and welcome the morning,
The warmth of the sunshine, or whisper of rain.
Let in the birdsong that heralds the dawning
Of day, with its pageant of colour again.
Glory to God for the freshness of morning,
Praise for its singing and stirring again.

Open your heart to the wonder of living,
The surge of creation about and above,
The joy of achievement, the gladness of giving,
The comfort of kindness, the sweetness of love.
Glory to God for the wonder of living,
Praise for its challenge, its laughter and love.

LOUIE HORNE

5 February

Your enjoyment of the world is never right, till every morning you awake in heaven; see yourself in your father's palace; and look upon the skies, the earth, and the air as celestial joys; having such a reverend esteem of all, as if you were among the angels. The bride of a monarch, in her husband's chamber, hath no such causes of delight as you.

You never enjoy the earth aright, till the sea itself floweth in your veins, till you are clothed with the heavens, and crowned with the stars: and perceive yourself to be the sole heir of the whole world, and more than so, because men are in it who are every one sole heirs as well as you. Till you can sing and rejoice and delight in God, as misers do in gold, and kings in sceptres, you never enjoy the world.

Yet further, you can never enjoy the world aright, till you so love the beauty of enjoying it that you are covetous and earnest to persuade others to enjoy it.

THOMAS TRAHERNE

6 February

My mother, nearing her end of days,
Said, in retrospective gratitude,
She being elsewhere bound,
"But it is a nice little world."
I too have found
Shelter here, birds, stars, waters, flowers, trees,
Kindness, dear human faces,
I too, *ils m'effroyent*, the eternal spaces.

KATHLEEN RAINE

7 February

There are flashes struck from midnights,
There are fire-flames noon-days kindle,
Whereby piled up honours perish,
Whereby swollen ambitions dwindle.
While just this or that poor impulse
Which for once had play unstifled
Seems the sole work of a life-time
That away the rest have trifled.

ROBERT BROWNING

8 February

Earth's crammed with heaven
And every common bush aflame with God.
But only he who sees takes off his shoes:
The rest stand round and pick blackberries.

ELIZABETH BARRATT BROWNING

9 February

What palaces we may build of beautiful thoughts...treasure
houses of precious and restful thoughts, which care cannot
disturb, nor pain make gloomy, nor poverty take away from us –
houses built without hands for our souls to live in.

JOHN RUSKIN

10 February

The moment of take-off was ecstatic. The dewy wing was suddenly covered with rivers of cold sweat running backward. The window wept jagged shiny courses of tears – Joy. We left the ground – I with Christian mantras and a great sense of destiny.

THOMAS MERTON

11 February

It is only in exceptional moods that we realize how wonderful are the commonest experiences of life. It seems to me sometimes that these experiences have an 'inner' side as well as the outer side we normally perceive. At such moments one suddenly sees everything with new eyes; one feels on the brink of some great revelation. It is as if we caught a glimpse of some incredibly beautiful world that lies silently about us all the time. I remember vividly my first experience of the kind when as a boy I came suddenly upon the quiet miracle of an ivy-clad wall glistening under a London street lamp. I wanted to weep and I wanted to pray: to weep for the Paradise from which I had been exiled, and to pray that I might yet be made worthy of it. Such moments are rare, in my experience. But their influence is permanent. They import a tinge of unreality into our normal acceptances; we suspect them for the dull and purblind things that they are.

There are analogous moments when one suddenly sees the glory of people. On some unforgettable evening one's friend is suddenly seen as the unique, irreplaceable, and utterly delightful being that he is. It is as if he had been freshly created. One is no longer concerned with his relation to oneself, with his pragmatic value. He exists wholly in his own right; his significance is eternal, and the essential mystery of his being is as fathomless as that of God Himself.

J. W. N. SULLIVAN

12 February

Heaven is what I cannot reach.
The apple on the tree,
Provided it do hopeless hang,
That is heaven to me.

The colour on the cruising cloud,
The interdicted land
Behind the hill, the house behind,
There paradise is found.

Her teazing purples, afternoons,
The credulous decoy,
Enamoured of the conjuror
That spurned us yesterday.

EMILY DICKINSON

13 February

I was in an Italian grocer's shop in Soho when it happened. It was
a Thursday afternoon and I was buying supper. I was gazing into
a large glass case, trying to decide between the dolcelatte and the
gorgonzola, when the whole business was knocked sideways by
an overwhelming feeling of the presence of God. It was so sweet
and strong that I was almost unable to keep standing. All I could
do was bow my head, as if investigating the prices per pound
from a nearer perspective, and hope I would emerge in one piece.

Sister Teresa of Avila lived with this sort of thing continuously,
but, being no saint, I can remember only one other instance in
my case. This time, again, it didn't happen in church as one
might hope and suppose; it happened at a board room lunch in
my office many years ago...The whole place was ablaze with
light in which I felt I would combust at any moment. And just
when it seemed safe enough to raise my head and try to look out
of the window, three white swans flew slowly past...

These visitations are not comfortable. But they are indescribably moving and they are a chief reason why some of us sinners working full-time in secular jobs in a thoroughly secular world cling to our beliefs in a way that might otherwise seem baffling even to ourselves.

ANN WROE

14 February

Whose wife is tender, wise, and true,
In fact, beloved, just like you,
Although he merits no such thing
Will live, as I do, like a king.

SA'DI

15 February

In the life of each of us, there is a place remote and islanded, and given to endless regret or secret happiness; we are each the uncompanioned hermit and recluse of an hour or a day; we understand our fellow of the cell to whatever age of history they may belong.

SARAH ORNE JEWETT

16 February

During the two years just before and after I was twenty I had two experiences which led to religious conversion. The first occurred when I was waiting at a bus stop on a wet afternoon. It was opposite the Odeon cinema, outside the station, and I was surrounded by people, shops, cars. All of a sudden, for no apparent reason, everything looked different. Everything I could see shone, vibrated, throbbed with joy, and with meaning. I knew that it had done this all along, and would go on doing it, but that usually I couldn't see it. It was all over in a minute or two. I climbed on to the bus, saying nothing to my friend – it seemed impossible to explain – and sat stunned with astonishment and happiness.

The second experience occurred some months later. I left my office at lunch-time, stopped at a small Greek café in Fleet Street to buy some rolls and fruit, and walked up Chancery Lane. It was an August day, quite warm but cloudy, with the sun glaringly, painfully bright, behind the clouds. I had a strong sense that something was about to happen. I sat on a seat in the garden of Lincoln's Inn waiting for whatever it was to occur. The sun behind the clouds grew brighter and brighter, the clouds assumed a shape which fascinated me, and between one moment and the next, although no word had been uttered, I felt myself spoken to. I was aware of being wholly accepted, accused, forgiven, all at once. The joy of it was the greatest I had ever known in my life. I felt I had been born for this moment and had marked time till it occurred.

MONICA FURLONG

17 February

At the end a big fellow, whose fearful looks could have inspired fear, told me, "Come to my house, I have something to honour you." I remained uncertain, not knowing whether I should accept or not, but the priest who was accompanying me said, "Go with him, Father, the people are very good." I went to his house, which was a half falling shack. He made me sit. From where I was seated the sun could be seen as it was setting. The fellow said to me, "Senor, you see how beautiful it is!" And we remained silent for some minutes. The sun disappeared. The man added, "I did not know how to thank you for all that you have done for us. I have nothing to give you, but I thought you would like to see this sunset. It pleased you, didn't it? Good evening." He then gave me his hand. As I was leaving I thought, "I have met very few hearts that are so kind."

JEAN CLAUDE DIETSCH

18 February

If we were really going about looking at this world, we would be moved a hundred times a day by the flowers at the side of the road, the people we meet, by all that brings us messages of our goodness and the goodness of all things.

ANDREW HARVEY

19 February

…When I read or hear
A perfect poem, brought into being
By someone else, someone perhaps
I've never heard of before – a poem
Bringing me pristine visions, music
Beyond what I thought I could hear,
A stirring, a leaping
Of new anguish, of new hope, a poem
Trembling with its own vital power –

Then I'm caught up beyond
That isolate awe, that narrow delight,
Into what singers must feel in a great choir,
Each with humility and zest partaking
Of harmonies they combine to make,
Waves and ripples of music's ocean,
Who hush to listen when the aria
Arches above them in halcyon stillness.

DENISE LEVERTOV

20 February

When you are old and grey and full of sleep
And nodding by the fire, take down this book,
And slowly read, and dream of the soft look
Your eyes had once, and of their shadows deep;

How many loved your moments of glad grace,
And loved your beauty with love false or true;
But one man loved the pilgrim soul in you,
And loved the sorrows of your changing face.

And bending down beside the glowing bars
Murmur, a little sadly, how love fled
And paced upon the mountains overhead
And hid his face amid a crowd of stars.

                                      W. B. YEATS

21 February

Look at this day...In it lie all the realities and verities of existence, the bliss of growth, the splendour of action, the glory of
power. For yesterday is but a dream, and tomorrow is only a
vision. But today well-lived makes every yesterday a dream of
happiness and every tomorrow a vision of hope.

                                FROM THE SANSKRIT

22 February

On one of the coldest moments of that spring, after she (Winifred
Holtby) had learned from a London specialist that she might
have two more years to live, she went for a walk past Clare
Leighton's cottage to a farm further up the hill. She felt tired and
dejected; her mind, still vigorously alive in her slow, impaired

body, rebelled bitterly against her fate. Why, she wondered, should she, at thirty-three, not yet in the fulness of her developing powers, be singled out for this cruel, unforeseen blow? She knew, for the constant demands of her friends had made it clear to her, that her life was infinitely valuable to others.

She thought of all the half-dead people who 'put in time' as though time were not the greatest gift in the universe, while she, who could use it so superbly, was soon to be deprived of it for ever; and she felt that her mind could hardly contain the anguish of that realization.

Just then she found herself standing by a trough outside the farmyard; the water in it was frozen and a number of young lambs were struggling beside it vainly trying to drink. She broke the ice for them with her stick; and as she did so she heard a voice within her saying, "Having nothing, yet possessing all things." It was so distinct that she looked round, startled. But she was alone with the lambs on the top of the hill. Suddenly, in a flash, the grief, the bitterness, the sense of frustration disappeared; all desire to possess power and glory for herself vanished away, and never came back.

VERA BRITTAIN

23 February

We walked together in the field. I can never forget the spot where it happened. I was barefoot on the green grass. My dad was beside me. It seemed like he was totally present to me and to all of nature. I remember feeling that his love, just then, was unconditional. And then something happened. It seemed like I connected with the trees, the wild flowers, the stones, the birds, the whole universe, my dad, and my own heart. A moment stood still in time. It was so powerful. That moment has stayed with me ever since. I became a child of nature. I connected with everything in the cosmos.

DANIEL O'LEARY

24 February

True as a mason's rule
And line can make them, the shafted columns rise
Singing like music; and by day and night
The unsleeping arches with perpetual voice
Proclaim in heaven: to labour is to pray.

DOROTHY SAYERS

25 February

Everyone suddenly burst out singing,
And I was filled with such delight
As prisoned birds must find in freedom
Winging wildly across the the white
Orchards and dark green fields;
On, on, and out of sight.

Everyone's voice was suddenly lifted;
And beauty came like the setting sun;
My heart was shaken with tears;
And horror drifted away...O but everyone
Was a bird; and the song was wordless;
The singing will never be done.

SIEGFRIED SASSOON

26 February

I have seen flowers come in stony places,
And kind things done by men with ugly faces,
And the gold cup won by the worst horse at the races:
So I trust too.

JOHN MASEFIELD

27 February

All great artists are masters at speaking through silence – the
object left out of the picture, the void in architecture, that pause
in the middle of a line of verse, the note withheld in music.
Recall for instance those four thundering Hallelujahs at the
climax of the Hallelujah Chorus – three of them, and then a
pause that seems to last for ever, and then the crashing fourth.
And in the throbbing silence is an unspoken Hallelujah as
piercing as the others.

COLIN MORRIS

28 February

There is a ceaseless music of the earth,
Tender and deep, for those who have ears to hear,
In mountains lone, and woods and murmuring trees,
And in the sky at midnight, when the stars
Chant without sound the song of all the spheres.

C. F. ANDREWES

29 February

On the way where the miles cannot be counted,
The name of God shall there be thy provision;
On the way where there is pitch darkness,
The name of God shall accompany and light thee;
On the way where nobody knoweth thee,
The name of God shall be there to recognize thee.

FROM THE SUKHMANI FROM THE SIKH TRADITION

March

The Grace of Suffering

1 March

Earth is a hard text to read. But what we can be certain of is that the screaming mob is insubstantial mist; in the clear sky, the thundering assertions fade to nothing. There the Lamb's song is sung, and what it celebrates is the apocalypse of a glory pain lays bare.

ROWAN WILLIAMS

2 March

The universe, however created, is a gigantic paradox, composed of joy and despair, of pain and delight, of beauty and ugliness, and inhabited by human beings who, likewise, are of amazing selflessness and heroism, and appalling cruelty and greed. Suffering is inevitably part of the human lot, and in some mysterious way, suffering seems built into the structure of the universe too. If one accepts the beauty and wonder, one must also accept the pain. Sooner or later in life, one begins to hear a constant undertone of what Wordsworth calls "the still, sad music of humanity".

JOAN FITCH

3 March

Grateful people are those who can celebrate even the pains of life because they trust that when harvest time comes the fruit will show that the pruning was not punishment but purification. I am gradually learning that the call to gratitude asks us to say 'everything is grace'. When our gratitude for the past is only partial, our hope for a new future can never be full...If we are to be truly ready for a new task in the service of God, our entire past, gathered into the spaciousness of a converted heart, must become the source of energy that moves us toward the future.

HENRI NOUWEN

4 March

If we are to begin to face the mystery of God – a mystery which can encompass the vastness of the universe, the depths of wickedness, the burning intimacies and promises of love and persons, then we must share in the risks of God – risks which include the possibilities of suffering, sin, and getting things wrong. The power of love is not having everything cut and dried, with reserve force to push the divine plan through. Such power could leave no room for the freedom which true love requires.

DAVID JENKINS

5 March

Only at a surface level is life merely a chronological sequence of events. There are certain happenings – the sudden loss of a parent in childhood, the death of a child or a partner, the breakdown of a marriage – that are so traumatic and life-changing that they seem to exist in a different dimension of time and are always deeply part of you. Yet what really matters is not what happens in this unpredictable world, but how we respond, what we make of what we are given, whether we have learned something about how even the starkest tragedy can be a means of grace that we might never have come to in any other way.

One of the deepest of Christian insights is that even in the worst of events God is present and there are possibilities of redemption. That is part of the meaning of the Cross: that good can be brought out of evil, that new life can emerge from an event that seems utterly final and devastating.

MICHAEL MAYNE

6 March

Healing is not achieved
Without some cost.
It may not mean the end of
Pain. Healing can hurt
Just like fresh wounds,
As pockets of poison are
Lanced, or lesions cut to
Allow more flexibility. For
Healing is not going back
To what one was before.
It is a growing on
To a new stage of being,
Through many deaths and
Resurrections being set free.

ANN LEWIN

7 March

God is to be found in the cancer, as in everything else. If He is
not, then He is not the God of the Psalmist who said, "If I go
down into hell, Thou art there also," let alone of the Christ who
knows God most deeply in the Cross. And I have discovered this
experience to be one full of grace and truth. I cannot say how
grateful I am for all the love and kindness and goodness it has dis-
closed, which I am sure were always there, but which it has taken
this to bring home…It has been a time of giving and receiving,
grace upon grace.

JOHN ROBINSON

8 March

It has been said that there can no poetry after Auschwitz, only silence. Silence alone can set things right between God and man. But, in a last talk given by Rabbi Nachum Yanchiken to Jewish students on the eve of the German invasion of Lithuania, he counselled them not simply to try to stay alive, but to "pour forth your words and cast them into letters – for words have wings, and they mount up to the heavenly heights and they endure for eternity."

ALAN ECCLESTONE

9 March

I believe in the sun even when it is not shining,
I believe in love even when feeling it not,
I believe in God even when He is silent.

ANON.

10 March

Never shall I forget that nocturnal silence which deprived me, for all eternity, of the desire to live. Never shall I forget those moments which murdered my God and my soul and turned all my dreams to dust.

ELIE WIESEL

11 March

Thibault pointed to a fallen tree beside them, sawn through the middle. "That dark ring there, it goes up and down the whole length of the tree. But you only see it where it is cut across. That is what Christ's life was: the bit of God that we saw. And we think God is like that, because Christ was like that, kind and forgiving sins and healing people. We think God is like that for ever, because it happened once in Christ. But not the pain. Not the agony at the last. We think that stopped."

Abelard looked at him, the blunt nose and the wide mouth, the honest troubled eyes. He could have knelt before him.

"Then, Thibault," he said slowly, "you think all this, all the pain of the world, was Christ's cross?"

"God's cross," said Thibault, "and it goes on."

HELEN WADDELL

12 March

The challenge of God does not only come to us through the word of a prophet. It is made visible in the presence of the poor whose desperation challenges us who are rich. In this new millennium we have begun to hear their cry and have mounted a political argument for remitting the Third World Debt that is grinding them down, but there is a much harder battle to be fought about the way the rich world deals with the refugees who are flooding into the affluent society of Europe. Sometimes it is fear of political persecution, sometimes ethnic cleansing, most often it is poverty that drives refugees to undertake journeys of terrifying hardship to get to a place where they believe that there is hope for the future instead of their deadly sense of despair.

They challenge us to look at the economic values that we are defending at the cost of their lives. When the tabloids encourage us to think that refugees are all scroungers, when we do not welcome the strangers but keep them in a ghetto or a detention centre, are we not stifling the voice of God as effectively as if we shot the prophets? Perhaps one of the ways of giving thanks to God for His prophets is to make sure that we do some of their work ourselves. Let us ask what justice demands of us as we gather round God's table and find a welcome here.

MICHAEL HARE DUKE

13 March

Under the heading of gifts, many people seem to include only very positive experiences. As a Christian, that's bound to worry me, because Jesus in Gethsemane said, "The cup which my Father hath given me shall I not drink it?" But it was a cup of suffering and sacrifice. Again, speaking personally, I'd have to say that nearly twenty-five years ago, at a time when I was going through it, when I hit a very painful patch of life – that time I now regard as the best thing that has happened to me. It was when Christ was betrayed that He did the best deed of His life. He took the thorns of that experience and twisted them into a crown of glory. The gift to do that is, I think, perhaps the greatest gift of all, the greatest grace of all.

ERIC JAMES

14 March

I believe that Good Friday people, like the *anawim*, the poor of God, are very specially loved by God, for He has called them to walk towards Him along a particularly narrow path, the road to Calvary, the same road as God's Son. I believe most deeply that they do not walk this path by chance and that they do not walk it in vain. I have no clever answer to the eternal 'Why?' of suffering, but I am convinced that whatever its outcome it is never without meaning.

SHEILA CASSIDY

15 March

The one who suffers wrong is stronger than the one who does wrong, for God is with the one who is suffering.

DOROTHEE SÖLLE

16 March

It is very good to have something to try to do with the pain. While it still remains an unmitigated evil, I can yet regard it somehow as a means to an end. I cannot describe the process very well, but I have found it to be one of somehow *absorbing darkness* – a physical or mental suffering of my own, or worse, of someone else's – into my own person, my own body, or my own emotions. We have to allow ourselves to be open to pain. Yet all the while we must resist any temptation to assent to its being other than evil. If we are able to do this, to act as it were, as a blotting paper for pain, without handing it on in the form of bitterness or of hurt to others – then somehow, in some incomprehensible miracle of grace, some at least of the darkness may be turned to light.

MARGARET SPUFFORD

17 March

When I had come by ill luck to Ireland – well, every day I used to look after sheep and I used to pray often during the day. The love of God and the fear of Him increased more and more in me and my faith began to grow and my spirit to be stirred up, so that in one day I would say as many as a hundred prayers, and I used to rise at dawn for prayer, in snow and frost and rain, because the Spirit was glowing in me.

PATRICK

18 March

The cross is a message of brokenness at the heart of the universe, and can only be received in the brokenness of being. It is a manifestation of power through weakness. That is what Luther meant when he spoke of the cross as the left hand of God. The straightforward, direct, forceful right hand may be outstretched in power and assertion, as it often is in conventional religion and conventional politics. But at the heart of the mystery of pain it is the left hand, the sinister, the indirect, the odd, and the strange, which comes into play.

KENNETH LEECH

19 March

In the flight into Egypt the holy family were refugees and exiles. They returned to the land where the Jews had been slaves for several centuries. Joseph had to be a migrant worker, a non-national to whom the most menial tasks are given even in our own day. Hence, for many years, Mary along with Joseph would have experienced tribulations by being foreign workers. In this too, they experienced personally the problems which many of the under-privileged people even in the rich countries have to face. They are the 'Third World' inside rich countries...It is a pity that popular devotions to Mary do not recall her in these experiences as a poor, courageous woman. She foreshadows the trials and struggles of women in our time too.

TISSA BALASURIYA

20 March

In Camus's great novel *The Plague*, a story of pestilence told by a doctor who stands up to death and says No, the author bears witness to those who died in the plague and tries "to state quite simply what we learn in times of pestilence, that there are more things to admire in men than to despise. The story could not be one of a final victory. It could only be the record of what had to be done, and what assuredly would have to be done again by all who, while unable to be saints, but refusing to bow to pestilences, strive their utmost to be healers."

That, I suggest, should be the response of the Church to the AIDS pandemic.

RICHARD HOLLOWAY

21 March

He who has suffered most knows many tongues.
He can be understood, he understands
The language of the countless ones
Who reach for sympathy with weak imploring hands...
There will be those who may require of you
Help to go on some first bewildering mile
With grief and pain. God will have need of you
As His interpreter that you may tell
Them of the hope ahead, of the healing peace,
And of His love. O, learn the language well.

ANON.

22 March

Aggrieved because I had no shoes,
I shuffled down the street,
Till someone cried, "There stumping goes
A man who has no feet."
Then was I instantly aware
That I from pain was free,
And thanked God the Compassionate,
For all He'd given me.

SA'DI

23 March

The friend that can be silent with us in a moment of despair or confusion, who can stay with us in an hour of grief and bereavement, who can tolerate not-knowing, not-curing, not-healing, and face with us the reality of our powerlessness, that is a friend who cares.

HENRI NOUWEN

24 March

Sitting with people in soul or spiritual pain requires real poverty
of spirit: to recognize one's helplessness, one's inability to provide
answers and give the ready-made solution. It, as it were, cuts the
ground from under us – under our need to be important and do
good. It leaves us naked and empty and vulnerable, and into this
emptiness the good Lord pours His compassion for those who are
wounded and hurting.

During my time in the hospice, we hosted an exhibition of
sculpture. One particular piece was of a figure standing like a
sentinel beside the entrance to the unknown. I keep a picture of
it always before me. The arms are outstretched almost to
breaking point, and the body is ridged and open with streaks of
red that stain your fingers when you touch them. Sharp pieces of
broken glass embedded in the figure can hurt and wound. These
symbolize the pain 'under the skin' which is experienced by the
person and shared by all who are in contact with him, especially
the loved ones. The closer the contact, the greater the pain.

AINE COX

25 March

O radiance, radiance of morning's new dawn,
O speak not a word, lest you miss what is born
From the womb of the Godhead creating with pain,
The nourishing gifts of the earth's fruit and grain.

"Is there one who is hearing?" God's heartbeat is pleading.
She is listening, listening, the bread she is kneading.
The silence enfolds her, keeps hidden its power,
O daughter, beloved, know this is the Hour!

O deep is the yearning, for healing she longs,
For a people's deliv'rance from oppression and wrongs.
While moulding the loaf – wheaten flour which earth yields –
She connects with her sisters still toiling in fields...

The silence is broken, there is rushing of wings,
The cry of the wild goose, exultant it sings –
"O rise up, daughter, love's power will unfold,
Revealing the healing of stories untold."

She is rushing through hillside, her sister she seeks,
In the mutual joy of encounter she speaks:
"God is listening, hearing all history's sorrow,
God is with me, creating, and birthing tomorrow ..."

MARY GREY

26 March

How often have I asked myself, and many ask themselves, "Why do children die?" And I never found an answer. But just recently, when I wasn't thinking about children at all any more, I became convinced that the only task in the life of each individual consists in strengthening love in himself, and in doing that, transmitting it to others and strengthening love in them also.

Our child lived so that those of us who were around him would be inspired by the same love, so that in leaving us and going home to God, who is Love itself, we are drawn all the closer to one another. My wife and I were never so close to each other as now, and we never before felt in ourselves such a need for love, nor such an aversion to any discord or any evil.

LEO TOLSTOY

27 March

Each time a baby or small child dies, we are reminded that the earth is not yet fully our home and that our life here is short – like a flower, like grass, like a butterfly. No matter how young the child, no matter how many hours or days or months we were given to love and to know that child, the pain seems unendurable, the wounds never quite seem to heal. What else can we do but trust, with the grieving parents, that in Jesus healing will be given, even though slowly and almost imperceptibly.

JOHANN ARNOLD

28 March

A loving and faithful priest who had had years of anxiety over the behaviour of one of his children said that countless people had said to him, "We'll pray for you." "But you know," he said, "it's just not enough. Not enough if we think we've done our bit once we've referred it to God. If we really pray then it involves far more than that…If we really pray we take a big risk because by so doing we are saying, 'Here am I, send me.'" God may take us at our word. Sometimes this will lead to practical action, however simple, like dropping in for a cup of tea. Even this can be a costly gesture, because by the very act of coming alongside someone who is suffering and laying ourselves open to their pain, we almost inevitably absorb some of that pain. In praying for a person experiencing black depression, we should not be surprised if we find ourselves rocked for a time by that same experience of blackness.

FRANCES DOMINICA

29 March

He stood before the court in nondescript clothes, no papers, no fixed address. The judge cleared his throat.

"Have you anything to say before I pass sentence?"

What might have been his answer, had the prisoner the gift of speech and the court the gift of hearing?

"I am condemned because your law allows no place for me. My crimes I freely admit: I am homeless, seeking shelter where I may rear my family in modest decency. I am stateless, seeking a country where I may belong by right in God's good earth. I am destitute, claiming a share of the wealth that is our common heritage. I am a sinner, needing aid from fellow sinners.

"You will dispose of me according to your law, but you will not so easily dispose of him who owns me citizen in his kingdom. He frowns on crimes your law condones: pride, selfishness, greed, self-righteousness, the worship of all things material and the refusal to acknowledge me as a brother."

EDMUND BANYARD

30 March

Don't grieve.
Anything you lose comes round in another form.
The child weaned from mother's milk
Now drinks wine and honey mixed.

RUMI

31 March

...to keep me from being too elated, a thorn was given me in the flesh, a messenger of Satan to torment me. Three times I appealed to the Lord about this, that it would leave me, but He said to me, "My grace is sufficient for you, for power is made perfect in weakness." So, I will boast all the more gladly of my weaknesses, so that the power of Christ may dwell in me. Therefore I am content with weaknesses, insults, hardships, persecutions, and calamities for the sake for Christ; for whenever I am weak, then I am strong.

PAUL

April

The Grace of Loving

1 April

Religion is no other than love – the love of God and of all people; loving God with all our heart and soul and strength, as having first loved us, as the fountain of all the good we have received and of all we ever hope to enjoy; and loving every soul which God has made, every soul on earth as our own soul.

JOHN WESLEY

2 April

Love is ever on the watch; it rests, but does not slumber, is wearied but not spent, alarmed but not dismayed; like a living flame, a blazing torch, it shoots upward, fearlessly passing through aught that bars its path. If anyone has this love, he will know what I mean. A loud cry in the ears of God is that burning love for Him in the soul which says, "My God, my love, you are all mine and I am all yours."

THOMAS A KEMPIS

3 April

Heaven and earth and all creation cry out to me that I must love. Everything tells me, With all your heart love the love that loves you; love the love which desires you, which has created you to draw wholly to itself. Therefore I desire never to stop drawing on this holy light and this ineffable goodness.

FRANCIS OF ASSISI

4 April

Love, and do what you will. If you hold your peace, of love hold your peace. If you cry out, of love cry out. If you correct, of love correct. If you spare, through love do you spare. Let the root of love be within. Of this root nothing can spring but what is good.

AUGUSTINE OF HIPPO

5 April

If thou wilt ask, "How good is he or she?" ask, "How much loves he or she?"

RICHARD ROLLE

6 April

The more we love, the better we are, and the greater our friendships are, the nearer we are to God.

JEREMY TAYLOR

7 April

Let none deceive another,
Or despise any being in any state.
Let none through anger or ill-will
Wish harm upon another.
Even as a mother protects with her life
Her child, her only child,
So with a boundless heart
Should one cherish all living being,
Radiating kindness over the entire world,
Spreading upwards to the skies,
And downwards to the depths unbounded.

BUDDHIST SCRIPTURES

8 April

Love is a going out of our own nature and an identification of ourselves with the beautiful which exists in thought, action, or person not our own.

PERCY BYSSHE SHELLEY

9 April

Love is the highest and only law of human life; and in the depth of his soul every human being – as we most clearly see in children – feels and knows this; he knows this until he is entangled by the false teachings of the world. This law was proclaimed by all – by the Indian as by the Chinese, Hebrew, Greek, and Roman sages of the world. I think this law was most clearly expressed by Christ who plainly said, In love alone is the law and the prophets.

LEO TOLSTOY

10 April

Of all things which wisdom provides to make life entirely happy, much the greatest is the possession of friendship.

EPICURUS

11 April

No medicine is more valuable, none more efficacious, none better suited to the cure of all our temporal ills than a friend, to whom we may turn for consolation in time of trouble, and with whom we may share our happiness in time of joy.

AELRED OF RIEVAULX

12 April

The story of Ruth ends characteristically with a sting in the tail for conventional wisdom. This woman, once a foreigner and a refugee, has a son, Obed. He was the father of Jesse, the father of David, Israel's greatest king, from whose descendants the Messiah was to come...Women who come to congratulate Naomi say to her, "Blessed be the Lord, who has not left you this day without next of kin; may his name be renowned in Israel. He shall be to you a restorer of life, and a nourisher of your old age; for your daughter-in-law who loves you, who is more to you than seven sons, has borne him." Naomi's daughter-in-law is more to her than seven sons. How far this is from conventional wisdom, yet how true it is! In the love of Ruth and Naomi, much is told about racial harmony, abiding faith, deepest commitment, to those who, as our Lord would say, have ears to hear.

MARTIN FORWARD

13 April

When she (Sri Saranda Devi) was weak and ill, and about to die, a disciple came to see her, and in a low voice the holy mother managed to give the personal guidance she was obviously needing. "If you want peace of mind," she said, "do not find fault with others. Learn rather to see your own faults. Learn to make the whole world your own; no one is a stranger, my child; the whole world is your own." In these few simple words she was stressing the underlying unity of all mankind; a unity in which there is no room for such words as 'yours' and 'mine', and no place for strangers.

KENNETH WALKER

14 April

In the Celtic tradition there is a beautiful understanding of love and friendship. One of the fascinating ideas here is the idea of soul love; the old Gaelic term for this is *anam cara*. *Anam* is the Celtic word for soul, and *cara* is the word for friend. So *anam cara* in the Celtic world was 'soul friend'. In the early Celtic Church a person who acted as a teacher, companion, or spiritual guide was called an *anam cara*. *Anam cara* was originally someone to whom you confessed, revealing the hidden intimacies of your life. This friendship was an act of recognition and belonging...

In everyone's life there is a great need for *anam cara*, a soul friend. In this love, you are understood as you are, without mask or pretension. The superficial lies and functional half-truths of acquaintance fall away. You can be as you really are. Love allows understanding to dawn, and understanding is precious.

JOHN O'DONOHUE

15 April

...I always think that the best way to know God is to love many things. Love a friend, a wife, something, whatever you like...But one must love with a lofty and serious intimate sympathy, with strength, with intelligence, and one must always try to know deeper, better, and more. That leads to God; that leads to un-wavering faith.

VINCENT VAN GOGH

16 April

Loving humility is a terrible force; it is the strongest of all things, and there is nothing like it.

FYODR DOSTOEVSKY

17 April

Then live my strength, anchor of weary ships,
Safe shore and land at last, thou for my wreck,
My honour, and my abiding rest,
My city safe for a bewildered heart.
What though the plains and mountains and the sea
Between us are, that which no earth can hold
Still follows thee, and love's own singing follows,
Longing that all things may be well with thee.
Christ who first gave thee for a friend to me,
Christ keep thee well, where'er thou art, for me.
Earth's self shall go, and the swift wheel of heaven
Perish and pass before our love shall cease.
Do but remember me, as I do thee,
And God who brought us on this earth together
Bring us together in His house of heaven.

HRABANUS MAURUS

18 April

With every true friendship we build more firmly the foundations
on which the peace of the whole world rests.

GANDHI

19 April

I say, such love is never blind; but rather
Alive to every the minutest spot
Which mars its object and which hate (supposed
So vigilant and searching) dreams not of.

ROBERT BROWNING

20 April

We are not here to multiply ourselves senselessly, but to increase
knowledge, to create beauty, and to increase love. Whatever helps
to do these things is right, whatever stands in their way is wrong.

J. B. PRIESTLEY

21 April

It is eighteen years ago, almost to the day –
A sunny day with the leaves just turning,
The touch-lines new-ruled – since I watched you play
Your first game of football, then, like a satellite
Wrenched from its orbit, go drifting away

Behind a scatter of boys. I can see
You walking away from me towards the school
With the pathos of a half-fledged thing set free
Into a wilderness, the gait of one
Who finds no path where the path should be.

That hesitant figure, eddying away
Like a winged seed loosened from its parent stem,
Has something I never quite grasp to convey
About nature's give-and-take – the small, the scorching
Ordeals which fire one's irresolute clay.

I have had worse partings, but none that so
Gnaws at my mind still. Perhaps it is roughly
Saying what God alone could perfectly show –
How selfhood begins with a walking away,
And love is proved in the letting go.

C. DAY LEWIS

22 April

...Hers the patience

Of one who made no claims, but simply loved
Because that was her nature, and loving so
Asked no more than to be repaid in kind.
If she was not a saint, I do not know

What saints are...

C. DAY LEWIS

23 April

Let me not to the marriage of true minds
Admit impediments: love is not love
Which alters when it alteration finds
Or bends with the remover to remove.
O, no, it is an ever-fixèd mark
That looks on tempests and is never shaken;
It is the star to every wandering bark,
Whose worth's unknown, although his height be taken.
Love's not Time's fool, though rosy lips and cheeks
Within his bending sickle's compass come;
Love alters not with his brief hours and weeks,
But bears it out even to the edge of doom:
    If this be error and upon me proved,
    I never writ, nor no man ever loved.

WILLIAM SHAKESPEARE

24 April

Let us be more loving and more indulgent towards one another. We are all so much in need of mutual love and help, and all our difficulties and sorrows are so insignificant in the face of eternity.

ALEXANDER ELCHANINOV

25 April

Do not hesitate to love and to love deeply. You might be afraid of the pain that deep love can cause. When those who love deeply reject you, leave you, or die, your heart will be broken. But that should not hold you back from loving deeply. The pain that comes from deep love makes your love ever more fruitful. It is like a plough that breaks the ground to allow the seed to take root and grow into a strong plant.

HENRI NOUWEN

26 April

We do know the value in an interior way of someone whose presence simply allows us to be, of a person around whom things bloom. They are not mindless optimists; they just have a way of being that seems to take some of the blockage out of the air, to uncomplicate us. They allow being. And that is how God creates, allowing things to be, evoking, calling them forth, seemingly without effort.

CLAIRE PREVALLET

27 April

Love is the vocation which includes all others.

THÉRÈSE OF LISIEUX

28 April

Here, only the twinkling of a hundred lamps lit the interior, allowing us to avoid tripping over a pair of Muslims prostrated on their prayer carpets near the entrance.

"And you have no objection to so many Muslims coming here and praying in your church?" I whispered. "We are all children of God," said Sister Tecla. "The All-Holy One brings us all together."

WILLIAM DALRYMPLE

29 April

An old woman once came to Ramakrishna and said, "I can't do any spiritual discipline, and I can't pray – I am completely hopeless." He smiled, took her hand, and asked her whom she loved most. The woman's face lit up, and she told him about her little grand-daughter. Ramakrishna told her to meditate on her grand-daughter, love her as divine, and her life would be filled with light...

Given the shortness of human life, and the infinite variety of possibilities, it is most important to choose one that corresponds to your deepest temperament and possibility and really follow it. All the masters agree that the essential thing is to master one way, one path, with all your heart right to the end, whilst remaining open and respecting the insights of all the others.

ANDREW HARVEY

30 April

If I speak in the tongues of mortals and of angels, but do not have love, I am a noisy gong or a clanging cymbal. And if I have prophetic powers and can understand all mysteries and all knowledge, and if I have faith so as to remove mountains, but do not have love, I am nothing...And now faith, hope, and love abide, these three, and the greatest of these is love.

PAUL

May

The Grace of Compassion

1 May

Sometimes in thinking and wondering at God's goodness to me, I have thought that it was because I sincerely loved His poor... I found Him in His poor and in a moment of joy I turned to Him. I have said, sometimes flippantly, that the mass of bourgeois smug Christians who denied Christ in His poor, made me turn to Communism, and that it was the Communists and working with them that made me turn to God...The experiences I have had are more or less universal. Suffering, sadness, repentance, love – we have all known these. They are easiest to bear when one remembers their universality, when we remember that we are all members of the mystical Body of Christ.

DOROTHY DAY

2 May

The poverty of the poor, the hunger of the hungry,
In such eyes as theirs I see a glow which means something.
Tell me, Shibli, how can I close my eyes to the world
And not wrong my own heart.

SALAH ABD AL-SABUR

3 May

Compassion is more than a feeling, an emotion...it is rooted in the mothering, womb-like compassion of God...Aung San Suu Kyi, under house arrest in Burma because of her resistance to the oppressive regime, speaks of compassion as the very strength that keeps her going...She speaks of it as "the quivering of the heart in response to others' suffering, the wish to remove painful circumstances from the lives of other beings."

MARY GREY

4 May

It is in the lived life of compassion – perhaps of being a 'buddy' to someone with AIDS – that we discover the truth of the Creeds, which are closed to the intellect alone. Perhaps our true Creed – what we really believe – is revealed not in what we say or think, but in what we do, indeed in our compassion.

ERIC JAMES

5 May

It is our sisterhood which we cherish and find empowering. In the words of Mother Teresa, an adopted daughter of Bengal, each of us – Hindu, Muslim, or Christian – wish in a humble way "to create something beautiful for God".

BENGALI WOMEN'S SUPPORT GROUP

6 May

Every time I give a piece of bread, I give it to Him. That is why we must find the hungry and the naked. That is why we are totally bound to the poor. The poor must know that we love them, that they are wanted. They themselves have nothing to give but love. We are concerned how to get this message of love and compassion across. We are trying to bring peace to the world through our work.

TERESA OF CALCUTTA

7 May

If we find this grace through our labour, with our fingers finding the loose thread in the garment, our ears late at night hearing the cries no one else hears, catching the milk in the pot as it begins to boil...or the grace of economy, the soup of leftovers...the slow opening, the listening, nodding, almost inarticulate, yet allowing articulation...the grace of the unspoken, spoken in movement, the hand reaches, the blanket is wrapped around, the arms hold this daily mulish grace, without which we do not wish to continue, and if we find this, we have something of our own. This is our secret grace, unnamed, invisible, surviving.

SUSAN GRIFFIN

8 May

God is as really our Mother as He is our Father. He showed this throughout when he said that sweet sound, "It is I." In other words, "It is I who am the strength and goodness of Fatherhood; I who am the wisdom of Motherhood; I who am light and grace and blessed love; I who am Trinity; I who am Unity; I who am sovereign goodness of every living thing; I who enable you to love."

JULIAN OF NORWICH

9 May

The saint, with true vision, conceives compassion for all the world, in east and west, and south and north, and so, knowing the Sacred Love, he will preach and proclaim it.

ACHARANA SUTRA

10 May

If we could understand history more clearly, we should discover that the most important influences shaping it were not emperors and kings, presidents and popes, generals and prime ministers, but the poor, the oppressed, the exploited and ignored, the criminals and prostitutes who in their affliction have found hope and trust in God, have let His love take hold of them and through the secret longings and prayers of their hearts, have sent waves of goodness and healing through creation.

GERARD HUGHES

11 May

No, it is not God's will that a few rich people enjoy the goods of this world and exploit the poor. No, it is not God's will that some people remain poor and abject for ever. No, religion is not the opiate of the people; it is a force that exalts the lowly and casts down the proud, that feeds the hungry and sends the sated empty away.

FROM A LETTER BY EIGHTEEN ROMAN CATHOLIC BISHOPS

12 May

When our churches have crumbled and our vestments rotted and the wind blows through the ruins of our ecclesiastical structures, all that will stand and have eternal significance are creative acts of compassion – the effective signs of the presence of the Kingdom.

COLIN MORRIS

13 May

We have wounds, but they take away our medicine.
We are hungry, but they took away our bread.
And here we suffer and there they are happy.
And here we weep and there they laugh.
And here we die and they are happy and laugh.
And we are poor and they are rich –
We without possessions,
They, owners, slaves, lord.

But we, we have more.
We have light, we have water, we have life.
Life, water, life are everlasting.
They will not perish with the dollar.
We have God.

HUMBERTO LIZARDI

14 May

What is sin? It is to turn a deaf ear to the cries of another person.

KAHLIL GIBRAN

15 May

Let us accept to sacrifice for others, especially at this time, to help refugees and displaced persons to find a home, to help them to rebuild and repair their damaged homes, to give them seeds and clothing, to share the little we have with them. For it is only when we lack love that we find nothing to share with others.

JOACHIM RUHANA

16 May

What do you think refugees do from morning to night? They spend most of their time telling one another the story of their lives. Their stories are anything but amusing, but they tell them to one another, really in an effort to make themselves understood. As long as there remains a determination to understand and to share one's understanding, perhaps we need not altogether despair.

IGNAZIO SILONE

17 May

The test of our relationship with God is not primarily our religious affiliation, assent to a creed or religious observance, but our relationships with others, especially to those in need. Political and social structures, which oppress the poor, the weak, and the powerless are the concern of God, who identifies Himself with their need, and they must therefore also be the concern of the Church.

GERARD HUGHES

18 May

People who are in need and are not afraid to beg give to people not in need the occasion to do good for goodness' sake. Modern society calls beggars bums and panhandlers. But the Greeks used to say that people in need are ambassadors of God. As God's ambassadors you should be given food, clothing, and shelter by those who are able to give it.

PETER MAURIN

19 May

Everything that Brigit would ask of the Lord was granted her at once. For this was her desire: to satisfy the poor, to expel every hardship, to spare every miserable man...She was simple towards God; she was compassionate towards the wretched; she was splendid in miracles and marvels: wherefore her name among created things is Dove among birds, Vine among trees, Sun among stars.

ON BRIGID OF KILDARE

20 May

Every noon at twelve
In the blazing heat
God comes to me
In the form of
Two hundred grams of gruel.

I know Him in every grain,
I taste Him in every lick,
I commune with Him as I gulp,
For He keeps me alive with
Two hundred grams of gruel.

I wait till next noon,
And now know He will come:
I can hope to live one day more,
For you made God come to me as
Two hundred grams of gruel.

I know that God loves me –
But not until you made it possible.
Now I know what you're speaking about,
For God so loves this world
That he gives His beloved Son
Every noon through you.

HYUN KYUNG CHUNG

21 May

It is impossible (fortunately) to have justice without compassion,
but it is possible (unfortunately) to have compassion without
justice. That sequence of justice and compassion is, therefore,
significant. We are back, in fact, with the distinction between, on
the one hand, individual good or evil and, on the other, systemic
good or evil. Where there is justice without compassion, there

will be anger, violence, and murder. A thirst for justice without an instinct for compassion produces killers. Sometimes they are simply believers in a Killer God. Sometimes they are assistant killers of a Killer God. But compassion without justice is equally problematic. In any unjust system, there are people needing immediate assistance. And even in a perfectly just system, there would still be those who would need compassion. But compassion, no matter how immediately necessary or profoundly human, cannot substitute for justice, for the right of all to equal dignity and integrity of life. Those who live by compassion are often canonized. Those who live by justice are often crucified.

JOHN DOMINIC CROSSAN

22 May

In a mysterious way, the people dying all over the world because of starvation and oppression, illness and despair, violence and war, become our teachers. In their immense pain and grief they ask us for solidarity not only in life but in death as well. Only when we are willing to let their dying help us to die well will we be able to help them to live well, because when we can face death with hope, we can live life with generosity.

HENRI NOUWEN

23 May

That I may weep for those who die of cold –
The ultimate cold within the heart of man.

EDITH SITWELL

24 May

If you cannot relieve, do not grieve the poor. Give them soft words if nothing else. Abstain from either sour looks or harsh words. Let them be glad to come, even if they go empty away. Put yourself in the place of every poor man and deal with him as you would God should deal with you.

JOHN WESLEY

25 May

One day last summer I saw a man sitting down by one of the piers, all alone. He sat on a log, and before him was a wooden box, on which he had spread out on a paper his meagre supper. He sat there and ate, with some pretence of human dignity, and it was one of the saddest sights I have ever seen.

DOROTHY DAY

26 May

In everyone there is something precious, found in no one else. So honour each person for what is hidden within him, for what he alone has and none of his fellows.

HASIDIC SAYING

27 May

All I do know is that life cannot be understood without much charity, cannot be lived without much charity. It is love, and not German philosophy, that is the true explanation of this world, whatever may the explanation of the next.

OSCAR WILDE

28 May

We all stood up in that simple basement chapel. We all held hands, prostitute and priest, pimp and nun, white and black, lay and religious. We all held hands, and in that moment I felt God breaking through and saying, "This is the Kingdom, this is My Kingdom."

EDWINA GATELEY

29 May

I have seen Christ
In the neglected face of an unloved boy.

I have seen Christ
In the gentleness and faith of an old man.

I have seen Christ
In the quick hands of a nurse
Who knew I needed her before I asked.

I have seen Christ
When my heart was breaking
In the compassionate eyes of a friend.

I have seen Christ
In the anguish of a mother
For her dying son.

I have seen Christ
In a dustman and a doctor.

God grant
That they may see Christ in me.

JOAN ROBERTSON

30 May

How does God's love abide in anyone who has the world's goods and sees a brother or sister in need and refuses help?

JOHN

31 May

May you always bear witness to the love of God in this world so that the afflicted and the needy will find in you generous friends and welcome you into the joy of heaven.

A BLESSING

June

The Grace of Giving

1 June

To give and give and give again
What God hath given thee,
To spend thyself nor count the cost,
To serve right gloriously
The God who gave all worlds that are
And all that are to be.

G. A. STUDDERT KENNEDY

2 June

The rabbi of Sassor once gave away the last money he had in his pocket to a man of ill repute. His disciples threw it up at him. He answered them, "Shall I be more finicky than God, who gave it to me?"

TALES OF THE HASIDIM

3 June

He caused me to think about the essence of giving cheerfully. One who gives gladly pays little heed to what he is giving. The desire and intention is to please and comfort the one to whom he gives it. And if the recipient accepts the gift gladly and gratefully, the gracious donor ignores the cost and the pain of the gift to himself, for delight and joy that has pleased and comforted one whom he loves.

JULIAN OF NORWICH

4 June

It is a barren prayer that does not go hand in hand with alms.

CYPRIAN OF CARTHAGE

5 June

There are those who have little and give it all. They are the believers in life, and the bounty of life, and their coffer is never empty.

KAHLIL GIBRAN

6 June

God looks unjust, but is not. God asks more from those to whom more is given. They are not greater or better; they have greater responsibility. They must give more service. Live to serve.

HELDER CAMARA

7 June

Sometime in your life hope that you might see one starved man, the look on his face when the bread finally arrives. Hope that you might have baked it, or bought it, or even kneaded it yourself. For that look on his face, for your meeting his eyes across a piece of bread, you might be willing to lose a lot, or suffer a lot, or die a little even.

DANIEL BERRIGAN

8 June

It is Jesus himself, through His words and actions, who teaches us the path which must be taken. It is enough for us to read into the concrete situation of today the parable of the Good Samaritan, and the cure of the leper. It is not for us to question why or how the illness was contracted.

EVARISTO ARIS

9 June

There is a kind of extravagance that belongs to any proper act of charity. Tillich called it 'holy waste', a term Dorothy Day would have appreciated. One thinks of Dorothy along with those great women of the Gospels, who often seemed to know with an extra sense, lacking in the more self-conscious men, the significance of the event unfolding in their presence. There was the woman who wasted a large quantity of expensive oil anointing Christ's body beforehand for His burial. Another woman bathed His feet with her tears and dried them with her hair. It was such women as these who remained on Calvary, watching their Lord on the cross. And to these women was entrusted the task of rushing from the empty tomb with the incredible news that He had risen. I think of Dorothy with such women. I know there are many – myself among them – who first heard the Good News through her.

ROBERT EHLBERG

10 June

The theology of liberation is one of the great gifts of the poor of Latin America to Christianity, as well as to the middle classes of the rich world to which I belong. It is a gift which is not used up, it nourishes me, as it nourishes the poor.

DOROTHEE SÖLLE

11 June

Without a rich heart, wealth is an ugly beggar.

RALPH WALDO EMERSON

12 June

The tradition of hospitality reached down to the humblest village. We could not pass even a widow's shack without being summoned in to partake of a handful of cardamon seeds, or a husk of coconut milk. And these delicacies were offered without complaint or excuse, for poverty was not felt as a moral failure or a vindictive act of fate. They had no expectations, they were at the bottom of the heap, and had learned not to hope for anything more.

HALLAM TENNYSON

13 June

Man is a being who does not dare to complete himself. He loves loving, but he is afraid to sacrifice; he loves giving, but he is afraid to lose.

LOUIS EVELY

14 June

Later in the week, someone gave us a radio, and one cold sunny morning we brought it over to Felicia (a poor woman who was penniless). She and the children were keeping warm in the janitor's flat. The janitor didn't mind two extra kids: she had twelve of her own, eight of them still living at home...Every now and then she would fall asleep on the bed...and the others would play around them. Maybe they didn't make much noise, because they didn't eat much. But the poor are like that. Always room, always enough for one more – everyone just takes a little less.

DOROTHY DAY

15 June

If I had only two loaves of bread, I would barter one for hyacinths to nourish my soul.

MOHAMMED THE PROPHET

16 June

Blessed are those who, when nothing can be done or said, do not walk away, but remain to provide a comforting and supportive presence – they will help the sufferer to bear the unbearable.

Blessed are those who recognize their own need to receive, and who receive it with graciousness – they will be able to give all the better.

Blessed are those who give without hope of return – they will give people an experience of God.

FLOR McCARTHY

17 June

In '41 Mama took me back to Moscow. There I saw our enemies for the first time: nearly twenty thousand German war prisoners were to be marched in a single column through the streets of Moscow. The pavements swarmed with onlookers, cordoned off by soldiers and police. The crowd was mostly women, Russian women with hands toughened by hard work, lips untouched by lipstick, and thin hunched shoulders which had borne half the burden of the war. Every one of them must have a father or a husband, a brother or a son killed by the Germans. They gazed with hatred in the direction from which the column was to appear...

All at once something happened to them. They saw German soldiers, thin, unshaven, wearing dirty blood-stained bandages, hobbling on crutches or leaning on the shoulder of their comrades...Then I saw an elderly woman in broken-down boots push herself forward and touch a policeman's shoulder, saying, "Let me through." She went up the column, took from inside her coat something wrapped in a coloured handkerchief and unfolded it. It was a crust of black bread. She pushed it awkwardly into the pocket of a soldier, so exhausted that he was tottering on his feet. And then suddenly from every side women were running towards the soldiers, pushing into their hands bread, cigarettes, whatever they had. The soldiers were no longer enemies. They were people.

YERGENY YEVTUSHENKO

18 June

What we do is very little, but it is like the little boy with a few loaves and fishes. Christ took that little and increased it. He will do the rest...What we do is so little that we may seem to be constantly failing. But so did He fail. He met with apparent failure on the Cross. But unless the seed fall into the earth and die, there is no harvest. And why must we see results? Our work is to sow. Another generation will be reaping the harvest.

DOROTHY DAY

19 June

There is a story about St Vincent de Paul, which says that on his death bed he spoke words like these to his community:

"When you grow tired of giving to others, when you are tempted to self-pity and begin to believe that others are taking advantage of you, that you are being asked to give more than is fair, then continue to give and maybe, sometime in the future, the poor will find it in their hearts to forgive you. For it is more blessed to give than to receive – and it is also a lot easier."

RONALD ROLHEISER

20 June

I am reminded of what Harold Talbot wrote about Thomas Merton's Asian journey: "He tipped taxi drivers like a Proustian millionaire. He was on a roll, a toot, a holiday from school. He was a grand seigneur, a great lord of the spiritual life. He woke people up, and enchanted them, and gave them tremendous happiness and a good laugh. People knew his spiritual quality. There was no question about it. Merton was not an object of scrutiny, he was an event."

We should so give ourselves to God that we are captured by God's recklessness and generosity the way Merton was, the way great souls always are.

RICHARD HOLLOWAY

21 June

Christian society in Britain has domesticated the Gospel. It is geared to loving God in moderation. We may give alms to the poor, visit the sick and the lonely, hold annual bazaars and flag days for those in need – in fact do any good works which do not threaten the pattern of our society. But to demand justice at the expense of people's comfort or security – that makes us trouble-makers.

SHEILA CASSIDY

22 June

The streets of Calcutta lead to everyone's door and the very pain, the very ruin of our Calcutta is the heart's witness to the glory that once was. I know you think you should make a trip to Calcutta, but I strongly advise you to save your airfare and spend it on the poor in your own country.

It is easy to love the people far away. It is not always easy to love those who live right next to us. There are thousands of people dying for a piece of bread. There are thousands more dying for a little bit of love, for a little bit of acknowledgment. People throughout the world may look different or have a different religion, education, or position, but they are all the same. They are people to be loved. They are people hungry for love.

TERESA OF CALCUTTA

23 June

The German writer Herman Hesse in his novel *Journey to the East* told of a great pilgrimage breaking up, and the travellers returning home disillusioned, asking what had happened to the dream, only to find that the pilgrimage did not require a physical leaving of home for exotic shrines: the challenge lay on the doorstep. Only they had not seen it before.

MARY GREY

24 June

John said to the crowds who came out to be baptized by him... "Bring forth fruits worthy of repentance."...And the crowds asked him, "What then shall we do?" In reply he said to them, "Whoever has two coats must share with anyone who has none; and whoever has food must do likewise." Even tax collectors came to be baptized, and they asked him, "Teacher, what should we do?" He said to them, "Collect no more than the amount prescribed for you." Soldiers also asked him, "And we, what should we do?" He said to them, "Do not extort money from anyone by threats or false accusation, and be satisfied with your wages."

GOSPEL ACCORDING TO LUKE, 3.7, 8, 10–14

25 June

I've travelled to the far corners of the earth and sat at the feet of some of the finest teachers of my generation. But I've never learned anything more profound than I did from that bunch of working class saints in the chapel in long ago Burry Port.

Each of them could be described as 'Christianity on two legs'; they were living examples of the power of God's love to change lives...Their language was action, their prayer love, and the Spirit manifested itself by turning a couple of dozen rough and ready people into a veritable army with a combined strength far greater than the sum of their individual parts. From them I learned the absolute priority of love over every other single aspect of Christian living, over doctrine and discipline alike. These people saw to it that my mother's poverty would not deprive her children of the necessities of life. I can't possibly count the number of times a garment, a school outing, some food, a Christmas present, magically arrived at exactly the right moment it needed to. The people of Israel were given manna and quails. Our provision was more varied but just as heaven sent.

LESLIE GRIFFITHS

26 June

If a beggar came to our door mother would never allow him to go away empty-handed. One day a very sturdy beggar came, and mother gave him alms. I protested, "Mother," I said, "that man looks perfectly fit; to give to such people is to encourage laziness. Those who give to the undeserving are the worse for it themselves. Does not the Gita tell us to consider that gift pure which is given at a fit place and time to a worthy person?" Mother listened, and then said very quietly, "Vinya, who are we to judge who is worthy and who is unworthy? All we can do is to regard everyone who comes to the door as God, and offer what is in our power. Who am I to judge him?" To this argument of my mother's I have not to this day been able to find a convincing reply.

VINOBA BHAVE

27 June

Give all thou canst.
High heaven rejects the lore
Of nicely calculated, less and more.

WILLIAM WORDSWORTH

28 June

Do all the good you can,
By all the means you can,
In all the ways you can,
In all the places you can,
At all the times you can,
To all the people you can,
As long as ever you can.

JOHN WESLEY

29 June

You are no longer strangers and aliens, but you are citizens with the saints and also members of the household of God, built upon the foundation of the apostles and prophets.

THE LETTER TO THE EPHESIANS 2.19

30 June

Love ever gives, forgives, outlives,
And ever stands with open hands.
And while it lives it gives.
For this is love's prerogative:
To give, and give, and give.

ANON.

July

The Grace of Forgiving

1 July

In its most profound sense forgiveness is about liberating people from the debilitating impasse of hurt and the desire to hurt in return. It is thus a process of re-membering which moves on from separation to community, from suspicion and confrontation to trust and mutuality. It is about creating space for perpetrators and victims to discover their common humanity and to covenant together for the sake of a safer, less violent future. In this sense, forgiveness is about training to inhabit this world together.

GEIKO MULLER-FAHRENHOLZ

2 July

Anger, pity, always, most, forgive,
It is the word which we surrender by,
It is the language where we have to live.

For all torn tempers, sulks and brawls at last
Lie down in huge relief as if the world
Paused on its axis. Sorrow does sound best

When whispered near a window which can hold
The full moon or its quarter. Love, I say,
In spite of many hours when I was cold

And obdurate I never meant to stay
Like that, or, if I meant to, I can't keep
The anger up. Our storms must draw away,

Their durance is not long. Almost asleep,
I listen now to winds' parley with trees
And feel a kind of comforting so deep

I want to share it. This unpaid for peace
Possesses me. How much I wish to give
Some back to you, but living's made of these

Moments when every anger comes to grief
And we are rich in right apologies.

ELIZABETH JENNINGS

3 July

If we have never sought, we seek Thee now;
Thine eyes burn through the dark, our only stars;
We must have sight of thorn-pricks on Thy brow,
We must have Thee, O Jesus of the Scars.

The heavens frighten us; they are too calm;
In all the universe we have no place.
Our wounds are hurting us; where is the balm?
Lord Jesus, by Thy Scars, we claim Thy grace.

If, when the doors are shut, Thou drawest near,
Only reveal those hands, that side of Thine;
We know today what wounds are, have no fear,
Show us Thy Scars, we know the countersign.

The other gods were strong; but Thou wast weak;
They rode, but Thou didst stumble to a throne;
But to our wounds only God's wounds can speak,
And not a god has wounds, but Thou alone.

EDWARD SHILLITOE

4 July

It was the power of forgiving love that made it possible for Abraham Lincoln to speak kind words about the people of the South even at a time when feelings were most bitter. Asked by a shocked bystander how he could do this, Lincoln replied, "Madam, do I not destroy my enemies when I make them my friends?"

ABRAHAM LINCOLN, QUOTED BY MARTIN LUTHER KING

5 July

Forgiveness does not mean ignoring what has been done or putting a false label on an evil act. It means, rather, that the evil act no longer remains as a barrier to the relationship. Forgiveness is the catalyst, creating the atmosphere necessary for a fresh start and a new beginning. It is the lifting of a burden or the cancelling of a debt. The words, "I will forgive you, but I'll never forget what you have done," never explain the real nature of forgiveness. Certainly one can never forget, if that means erasing it totally from one's mind. But when we forgive, we forget in the sense that the evil deed is no longer a mental block impeding a new relationship. Likewise, we can never say, "I will forgive you, but I won't have anything further to do with you." Forgiveness means reconciliation, a coming together again.

MARTIN LUTHER KING

6 July

When, through my tears, I began to tell Jesus something of the years during which I betrayed Him, He lovingly placed His hand on my mouth in order to silence me. His concern was that I should muster enough courage to pick myself up again to try to carry on walking, in spite of my weaknesses, and to believe in His love, in spite of my fears.

CARLO CARETTO

7 July

For most of us, whatever the circumstances, forgiveness is something that has to be worked at and is a process which continues for a long time. In its initial impact any deep injury to ourselves is a kind of bereavement and leaves us not only with feelings of pain and anger, but also of deep insecurity. Because of this, forgiveness is not a quick task which is over and done with once and for all. Rather is it a matter of living with a difficult situation and trying deliberately to feed constructive thought into it so that it begins to contribute to our growth rather than to detract from it.

ANN BIRD

8 July

Sleep, and if life was bitter to thee, pardon;
If sweet, give thanks; thou hast no more to live,
And to give thanks is good, and to forgive.

ALGERNON CHARLES SWINBURNE

9 July

There is all the difference in the world between forgiving and excusing. Forgiveness says, "Yes, you have done this thing, but I accept your apology, I will never hold it against you and everything between us will be exactly as it was before." But excusing says, "I see that you couldn't help it or didn't mean it, you weren't really to blame." If one was not really to blame, then there is nothing to forgive. In that sense forgiveness and excusing are almost opposites.

Real forgiveness means looking steadily at the sin, the sin that is left over without any excuse, after all allowances have been made, and seeing it in all its horror, dirt, meanness, and malice, and nevertheless being wholly reconciled to the one who has done it. That, and only that, is forgiveness, and that we can always have from God if we ask for it.

C. S. LEWIS

10 July

The spiritual person hides the faults of others, as God protects the world, as Christ washes our sins in His blood, as the Mother of God stretches the veil of her tears over the human race.

OLIVIER CLÉMENT

11 July

Without being forgiven, released from the consequences of what we have done, our capacity to act would, as it were, be confined to a single deed from which we could never recover; we would remain the victims of its consequences for ever.

HANNAH ARENDT

12 July

When people hate, its power engulfs them and they are totally consumed by it...Keep struggling against hatred and resentment. At times, you will have the upper hand; at times you will feel beaten down. Although it is extremely difficult, never let hatred completely overtake you. Never stop trying to live the commandment of love and forgiveness.

NAIM ATEEK

13 July

Time after time I have forgiven a person both by word and in my heart, only to find that same person within an hour committing that very same offence once more. Similarly, there have been many occasions when I have been forgiven, yet have found myself soon afterwards on the point of committing the same offence once again. The matter of the dispute has still been lodged somewhere inside me and is going to take long time – perhaps seventy times, a lifetime – before it is dissolved.

The conclusion I am bound to come to, therefore, is that when we speak of forgiveness we should have in mind not so much a series of discrete acts (though it is that) as a continuous, lifelong condition. There is no moment when one is not in need of forgiveness nor any moment when one does not need to be forgiving.

DONALD NICHOLL

14 July

It hurts too much to hate. Hating is a burden to me. For me to survive and to be useful to myself and to the community I serve I find it easier to forgive. You may dislike what someone, or the community, does to you. But I cannot cope with hating, even though I get angry with what is done to me. But in the end I find it easier to discover ways of forgiving a person what they have done to me than to continue to hold something against them.

Because of that I get into hot water. People condemn me, yet I find it difficult to be other people's judge and jury. You see, because of my own sin, I see how easy it is to do wrong things. Because I am a follower of Him who said, "The person who is without sin cast the first stone," I try to live by forgiveness.

SYBIL PHOENIX

15 July

A clear alternative is placed before us – the love of power, which produces and maintains separation, leading to death; or the power of love, which travails for the breaking down of separation and for the reunion of the oikoumene, that we may all share the endless life of the open city. The power of love is hope in action – action founded on the divine promise, "Behold, I am making all things new."

PHILIP POTTER

16 July

"In memory of the men of this college, who, coming from a foreign land, entered into the inheritance of this place, and, returning, fought and died for their country in the war, 1914–1918."

MEMORIAL IN THE CHAPEL OF NEW COLLEGE, OXFORD

17 July

The bodhisattva loves all living beings as if each was his only child.

THE BUDDHA

18 July

Yet all is well; he has but passed
To life's appointed bourne
And alien tears will fall for him,
Pity's long broken urn,
And his mourners will be outcast men
And outcasts always mourn.

OSCAR WILDE

19 July

Even news about soldiers coming to Biram (in Galilee) could not unsettle father…If need be, these Jews from Europe could settle in our village and farm the land that lay open beside our own fields. But my brother Ruldah shocked us all by bringing home a rifle – one of the two or three guns in all of Biram.

When father saw the rifle he erupted in a rare show of anger. "Get it out of here! I won't have it in my house. We do not use violence ever – even if someone hurts us …"

"But father," Ruldah persisted anxiously. "Why do the soldiers carry guns?"

Slipping his arm around Ruldah's shoulders, father replied, "For centuries our Jewish brothers have been exiles in foreign lands. They were hunted and tormented – even by Christians. They have lived in poverty and sadness. They have been made to fear and sometimes when people are afraid, they have to carry guns."

"But how do we know the soldiers won't harm us?" Ruldah pressed him.

Father smiled, and all the tension seemed to relax. "Because the Jews and Palestinians are brothers – blood brothers. We share the same father, Abraham, and the same God. We must never forget that. Now get rid of your gun."

ELIAS CHACOUR

20 July

In the film story of Gandhi there is an unforgettable scene between Gandhi, ill from fasting, and a despairing Hindu. "I'm going to hell!" said the Hindu. "Why?" whispered Gandhi. "Because I killed a child. I killed a child because they (the Muslims) killed my son." "I can show you a way out of hell," Gandhi said. "Go, find a boy, a Muslim boy the age of your own son. Take him in, raise him as your own. But," Gandhi looked straight into the man's eyes, "be sure you raise him as a Muslim."

GANDHI, QUOTED BY GWEN CASHMORE AND JOAN PULS

21 July

To forgive and to be forgiven are two sides of the same precious coin whose value is freedom, self-fulfilment, peace. A few years ago in Hong Kong I visited the grave of an uncle of mine who'd spent much of his long life there as a Jesuit priest. He'd been upset with me, justifiably so, over the break-up of my marriage. We hadn't been in touch in his last years.

After flowers had been placed, a prayer said, and some pictures taken for the family back home, my Jesuit host and I shared a few beers. "I really want to believe," I said, "that he's forgiven me."

Father Michael's eyes twinkled over the rim of his glass. "Well, if he hasn't, then he's not in the place where we know he is."

DENIS TUOHY

22 July

A brother who had sinned was expelled from the church by the priest. Whereupon Abba Bessarion rose and went with him, saying, "I too am a sinner."

ABBA BESSARION

23 July

It was at a church service in Munich that I saw him, the former SS man who had stood guard at the shower room in the processing centre at Ravensbruck…And suddenly it was all there – the roomful of mocking men, the heaps of clothing, Betsie's pain-blanched face.

He came up to me as the church was emptying, beaming and bowing…His hand was thrust out to shake mine. And I, who had preached so often the need to forgive, kept my hand at my side.

Even as the angry, vengeful thoughts boiled through me, I saw the sin of them. Jesus Christ had died for this man, was I going to ask for more? Lord Jesus, I prayed, forgive me and help me to forgive him…

As I took his hand the most incredible thing happened. From my shoulder and along my arm and through my hand a current seemed to pass from me to him, while into my heart sprang a love for this stranger that almost overwhelmed me.

And so I discovered that it is not on our forgiveness any more than on our goodness that the world's healing hinges, but on His. When He tells us to love our enemies, He gives, along with the command, the love itself.

CORRIE TEN BOOM

24 July

In May 1945 I was just liberated from the concentration camp at Gunskirchen, and some of my friends, who were in better physical shape than I, found a most sadistic Nazi sergeant and strung him up. There was a catharsis going on, and I was at that point all of fifteen years old, and there was that bit of me which felt that there was something right about it. But there was that bit of me, and it has not left me, which scared me, because I knew that this was really responding in kind, and that if you want to consider yourself a civilized human being you cannot go up and down wreaking vengeance. That was what this was. But I can understand the enormously strong power that would give me something to pay back the suffering, the humiliation.

HUGO GRYN

25 July

In 1984 I was invited to the commemoration in Marzobotto, a commune to the south of Bologna, of the massacre that had taken place there forty years previously of some two thousand citizens. One of the abiding memories of my visit is that if ever one of the guests at the commemoration happened to speak of 'the massacre by the Germans', then one of the citizens of Marzobotto present would politely correct them, that it was not the Germans but the Nazis who had been responsible. The reason why the people of the commune were always so careful to make the correction was because on the day of the massacre one young German soldier had refused to take part and had himself been shot in consequence. That young soldier, in his stark loneliness, had saved the good name of his nation.

DONALD NICHOLL

26 July

It is wrong to say that only the victims can forgive. The victims have their history too, and they make history. Their pain influences the coming generations, especially if it is never openly addressed. It is essential to take the intergenerational impact of suffering into account and to involve the coming generations in the processes of forgiveness. For genuine forgiveness is about unburdening the past in order to inaugurate less painful relationships in the future.

GEIKO MULLER-FAHRENHOLZ

27 July

If it should happen one day – and it could be today – that I become a victim of the terrorism that now seems to encompass all foreigners living in Algeria, I would like my community, my church, my family, to remember that my life was given to God and to Algeria, and that they accept that the sole Master of all life was not a stranger to this brutal departure.

I would like when the time comes to have a space of clearness that would allow me to beg forgiveness of God and of my fellow human beings, and at the same time to forgive with all my heart the one who will strike me down.

I could not desire such a death. It seems to me important to state this. How could I rejoice if the Algerian people I love were indiscriminately accused of my murder? For this life lost, I give thanks to God. In this thank you I certainly include you also, my last minute friend who will not have known what you are doing. I commend you to the God in whose face I see yours. And may we find each other, happy 'good thieves' in Paradise, if it please God the Father of us both.

CHRISTIAN DE CHERGE

28 July

I realized that if (after being the victim of a letter bomb sent from South Africa) I became filled with hatred, bitterness, self-pity, and desire for revenge, I would remain a victim for ever. It would consume me. It would eat me alive. God and people of faith and hope enabled me to make my bombing redemptive – to bring life out of death, good out of evil. I was enabled to grow in faith, and in commitment to justice and compassion.

MICHAEL LAPSLEY

29 July

Dear Pupils,
As midnight tolled last Friday your headmaster and my husband (who had been stabbed outside his school) lost his fight for life. Your sweet letters to me recognized that in that moment, the world was deprived of a man of great strength, tenderness, and profound understanding…Through your loving letters I can see how you care about other people. I can see that you understand the difference between right and wrong and your belief that love should overcome hatred. Your head teacher's, my husband's, death will not be in vain if you grow up with these ideals rooted firmly in your hearts…

Violence is not a knife in the hand. It grows, like a poisoned tree, inside people who, unlike yourselves, have not learned to value other human beings. Now I trust you to work as hard as you can in school and at home to create a world in which goodness is never again destroyed by evil.

FRANCES LAWRENCE

30 July

Only time will determine the effectiveness of the Truth and Reconciliation Commission process. Its stated aims are to produce a record of the violations of the past, and make recommendations to prevent them ever happening again; to acknowledge the suffering of the victims and assist in their re-habilitation, to offer amnesty to past perpetrators and to facilitate the healing and reconciliation of the nation...

In one case a police officer who masterminded the butchering of a number of families in an attack on a rural village stood and faced his victims. "I can never undo what I have done," he said, "I have no right to ask your forgiveness, but I ask that you will allow me to spend my life helping to rebuild your village and put your lives together." It is in moments like these that anger at the unrepentant is superseded by something more: out of the horrors of the past, the Commission makes space for grace, and the potential for newness in South Africa shines through...

Victims do seem to have been helped by telling their stories. Numbers of them have said that they now feel able to move forward with their lives. Most important has been the 'reverencing' of their suffering. "Today," said an old black man, "the nation has cried my tears with me."

PETER STOREY

31 July

South Africa has moved into the future with one big leap forward, developing a politics of forgiveness in a more sophisticated manner than any other country. It now needs to show how citizens can be empowered to join in that process at the grassroots and help create a multi-faith and multi-cultural society across all the former divisions. It if begins to do this it may well become one of the key players in this twenty-first century.

BRIAN FROST

August

The Grace of Choosing

1 August

When we take risks, when we let the props go and give ourselves up to the struggle, God's grace is more radiant than at other times. Grace empowers us to choose rightly in what seems to be the most choice-less of situations, but it does not and will not determine that choice.

So while grace is a gift from God, the power of grace flows more fully when we choose to act in harmony with the divine will. In practical terms, this means staying in a situation, being willing to confront it as it is, remaining responsible for the choice one makes in response to it, while at the same time returning to God's grace, protection, and guidance as the ground for one's choices and behaviour.

STANISLAUS KENNEDY

2 August

If a man happens to be thirty-six years old, as I happen to be, and some great truth stands before the door of his life, some great opportunity to stand up for that which is right and that which is just, and he refuses to stand up because he wants to live a little longer and he is afraid his home will get bombed, or he is afraid that he will lose his job, or he is afraid he will get shot...he may go and live until he's eighty, and the cessation of breathing in his life is merely the belated announcement of an earlier death of the spirit.

A man dies when he refuses to stand up for that which is right.

A man dies when he refuses to take a stand for that which is true.

So we are going to stand up right here...letting the world know that we are determined to be free.

MARTIN LUTHER KING

3 August

Some years ago I visited this venerable figure in Atlanta, Martin Luther King Senior, the head of a household where violent death has called so many times. Yet this was not a bitter person, but a Christian leader who talked of his duty to forgive, of the task of reconciliation. We walked to the grave of his famous son, and stood by the stone with its inscription, "Free at last!"

"Do you know who I am, rabbi?" the old man asked, leaning on my shoulder. "I am Abraham, and there lies my son Isaac."

ALBERT FRIEDLANDER

4 August

A Buddhist monk was once asked, "What is sin?" Very often in the East a question is answered by a question, it is part of their wisdom, a result of deep meditation. The monk asked the pupil to open his hands wide.

"What can you do with your open hands?" The reply was, "I can arrange flowers, embrace a loved one, work, and in general do all manner of good things."

Then the monk went on, "Now, close your hands slowly, starting with each finger. What have you now? What can you do?"

The pupil did as he was told and stared at his two fists. He realized the terrible things he could do and finally said, "I can hurt, injure, even kill someone." "That," said the Buddhist monk, "is what sin is."

BUDDHIST MONK, REFERRED TO BY PETER WINDRAM

5 August

The truth of life is that life is not a given. We are its co-creators. The globe is in our hands. Life is at our mercy. We must be impelled by the vision that inspired it, committed to the glory that created it, and confident in the beauty that sustains it. To say, 'I believe,' is to say that my heart is in what I know but do not know, what I feel but cannot see, what I want and do not have, however much I have. To say 'I believe' is to say yes to the mystery of life.

JOAN CHITTISTER

6 August

On 6 August 1985 I was present in Hiroshima with many thousands as the Japanese commemorated the dropping of atom bombs on Nagasaki and Hiroshima...We met with several disfigured survivors of that horrible obscenity perpetrated forty years earlier and we were devastated. I asked what purpose was being served by recalling such a traumatic experience and I was deeply touched when the Japanese said without bitterness or rancour that they commemorated it because this awful thing had happened to them and they did not want it ever again to happen to others. I found their willingness to forgive and their concern for humankind quite staggering.

DESMOND TUTU

7 August

Today we live in a time in which old forms are passing away. In the midst of revolutionary change, we who have so carefully plotted the way in which we would change the world found ourselves overtaken by events. But before us lie extraordinary opportunities. We need to dream anew, to draw upon our senses and passions, our thoughts and imagination, to see the world as God intended it, so that we can be agents of its transfiguration.

The dream is real. May we, by the grace of God, and through the intercession of Our Lady of the Magnificat, Blessed Conrad Noel and all the Saints, both dream it and be partakers of it, now and in the age to come.

JOHN ORENS

8 August

It is the duty of the Church to become, in Desmond Tutu's words, the voice of the voiceless poor and the voice of the voiceless God. Prophecy, by definition, is rarely moderate in tone. In order to attract attention, it shocks. It is a kind of spiritual terrorism, designed to make people hear the voices of those they never meet, see people they never encounter, endlessly calling society to repentance and renewal.

RICHARD HOLLOWAY

9 August

Our deepest fear is not that we are inadequate. Our deepest fear is that we are powerful beyond measure. It is our light, not our darkness, that most frightens us. We ask ourselves: Who am I to be brilliant, gorgeous, talented, and fabulous? Actually who are you not to be? You are a child of God. Your playing small doesn't save the world. There's nothing enlightened about shrinking so that other people won't feel insecure around you. We were born to manifest the glory of God that is within us. It's not just in some of us; it's in everyone. And as we let our light shine we unconsciously give other people permission to do the same. As we are liberated from our own fear our presence automatically liberates others.

NELSON MANDELA

10 August

Otherworldliness in theology often manifests itself as extreme worldliness in practice, because it encourages a sharp division between the realms of spirit and matter, between religion and world affairs. Since the former cannot influence, question, or shape the latter, they end up co-existing peacefully.

KENNETH LEECH

11 August

No liberation theology can be developed in the United Kingdom today without a profound sensitivity to the question of racism as evil, and multi-culturalism as a liberating power for good.

AUSTIN SMITH

12 August

Christianity is not primarily a philosophy but a crusade. As Christ was sent by the Father, so He sends His disciples to set up in the world the Kingdom of God. His coming was a declaration of war – a war to the death against the powers of darkness. He was manifested to destroy the works of the devil. Hence when Christians find in the world a state of things that is not in accord with the truth which they have learned from Christ, their concern is not that it should be explained, but that it should be ended. In that temper we must approach everything in the relations between the races that cannot be reconciled with the Christian ideal.

J. H. OLDHAM

13 August

If you are neutral in situations of injustice, you have chosen the side of the oppressor. If an elephant has his foot on the tail of a mouse, and you say that you are neutral, the mouse will not appreciate your neutrality.

DESMOND TUTU

14 August

I never trust people who say they have no view and never vote, and are neutral in matters. Some hacks tell you that, and I think they are less good for it. I think that you must be driven, outraged by hypocrisy, by lying, by deceit, and by corruption, and you must be prepared to be impressed and moved, and able to cry and laugh and respect what is good.

JON SNOW

15 August

For my part I have come increasingly to see that Mary is utterly central to a religion of the Word made flesh. Jesus is born of the Spirit of God, but he is also bone of her bone, and flesh of her flesh. In her entire openness to God, she becomes the bearer of Christ, and the chattel of Divine Love for the world.

In accepting her calling then, she has a special relationship to God; and in becoming the Mother of Jesus she has a unique bond with her Son...We not only 'behold the man'; we behold the handmaid of the Lord, who, as the Mother of Jesus, so faith-fully carried out the divine will...Mary, then, is for believers a patron of faith. She points us to Jesus the Lord who is 'Mary's Son'. We may say more than that. Since Christians form the Body of Christ, Mary the Mother is also – like the Jerusalem that is from above – the Mother of all.

JOHN NEWTON

16 August

When Cardinal Manning made his great plea to society to show compassion to the 'worthless' among them, he put aside all restraint.

"If then the worthless are what they are because the society of today has wrecked them, what is society doing, or willing to do, to redeem and save the worthless? None are so bad that there is not still hope...Human sympathy, kind care, personal service, patient goodwill are policies which never fail. If through fault of ours, however remotely or indirectly, by commission or omission, they are outcasts, let us now begin and try to bring them back to what once they were. The memory of their childhood is not dead with them; and if it be only a gleam of innocence long lost, it is also a throb of a higher life, not yet extinct for ever."

EDWARD MANNING

17 August

I join with all, believers or not, who see the abuse of the earth that has been entrusted to the human race, together with the unjust distribution of its products and the exploitation of the poor nations by the rich, as the supreme evils and dangers, threatening our very existence.

ROBERT MURRAY

18 August

Where, in heaven's name, can we discover any hint that it is in a Divine purpose that the wide bounty of the universe has been designed chiefly to benefit twenty per cent of its inhabitants?

BARBARA WARD

19 August

Freedom of choice for me is all very well, but not if its necessary condition is absence of choice for somebody else. Of course people have always been selfish because people have always been sinful. But things are in a bad way when, far from being recognized as sinful, selfishness is turned into a publicly acceptable principle of social and personal policy.

MARK SANTER

20 August

The inspired and benevolent author of Christianity taught neither intolerance nor persecution. The doctrines He laid out …hold out mercy to the contrite and to the humble, and eternal happiness to the good. For my own part it is long since I left off bewildering myself with dogmas and creeds, and I feel pity for those who do so.

THOMAS BEWICK

21 August

The growing good of the world is partly dependent on unhistoric acts; and that kings are not so ill with you and me as they might have been is half owing to the number who lived faithfully a hidden life, and rest in unvisited tombs.

GEORGE ELIOT

22 August

A true lover of God can inspire his brothers and sisters with a desire to return to their home in Him, but they themselves, step by step, must make the actual journey.

PARANAHATSU YSGANANDA

23 August

Trade with the gifts God has given you. Bend your minds to holy learning that you may escape the fretting moth of littleness of mind that would wear out your souls. Brace your wills to action that they may not be the spoil of weak desires. Train your hearts and lips to song which gives courage to the soul. Being buffeted by trials, learn to laugh. Being reproved, give thanks. Having failed, determine to succeed.

HILDA OF WHITBY

24 August

Spiritual writers spend quite a lot of time talking about 'detach-ment'...No doubt there are souls who for their own protection must eschew all human affection if they are to cleave to God in purity of heart. I am not one of them. For me, detachment is only real if it involves loving: loving to the fullest extent of one's nature but recognizing at the same moment that such love is set in the context of a supernatural love of God. Then, when the moment of sacrifice, of parting, comes, one has a worthwhile offering to make...[I]t has some meaning, like the precious oint-ment poured out at the feet of Christ. And it is costly too.

TREVOR HUDDLESTON

25 August

We cultivate, but get no food.
We work on the land, but go hungry.
We labour in the fields, but the landlords suck our blood.
We need to struggle together –
We get nowhere without struggle.

DALIT SONG

26 August

Those who invented neither gunpowder nor compass,
Those who never knew how to conquer steam or electricity,
Those who explored neither sea nor sky,
But those without whom the earth would not be earth.

AIMÉ CESARE

27 August

It is relatively easy to see what is wrong and to reflect on it in
faith; it can be much harder to take that reflection into action,
and yet this is what we are called as Christians to do, and as
Christian women we have a duty to take the fruits of our volun-
tary action into the political sphere.

CATHERINE SHELLEY

28 August

It is not your obligation to complete your work, but you are not
at liberty to quit.

THE TALMUD

29 August

To choose the world is not merely a pious admission that the
world is acceptable because it comes from the hand of God...To
choose the world is to choose to do the work I am capable of
doing, in collaboration with all my brothers and sisters, to make
the world better, more free, more just, more liveable, more
human.

THOMAS MERTON

30 August

We shouldn't be surprised, if we seek to follow Jesus, that it will cost us our lives. It cost Him His life. And we shouldn't be afraid as Christians to join other people of good will. Jesus Himself chose so frequently not to make common cause with the religious people of His day. He chose to make common cause with people of good will who sought a new society, a vision, a hope for the future.

MICHAEL LAPSLEY

31 August

Thank God, our time is now,
When wrong comes up to meet us everywhere,
Never to leave us until we take
The longest stride of soul man ever took.
Affairs are now soul size.
The enterprise is exploration into God.
Where are you making for?
It takes so many years to wake,
But will you wake, for pity's sake?

CHRISTOPHER FRY

September

Our Lady of Grace

1 September

We are inheritors of a great and healthy tradition with regard to Our Lady, and in that tradition she was never separated from her Son. Have we ever considered what a wonderful thing it is that we still have in everyday usage a blessing or greeting such as 'May God and Mary be with you'? Seldom in speech was God referred to without Our Lady also being mentioned. Especially in the Passion there was deep sympathy with the suffering Mother.

I have myself seen old men in Gaeltecht raise their caps and bow their heads at the mention of Our Lady, just as the Angel bowed at the Annunciation. He who would mention her name would say, 'Praise and all honour to her', and if the phrase were omitted, some old person would be sure to interject it. In the words of Fergal Og Mac av Bhaird, a poet of the late sixteenth century: "Abandon not Mary, the Mother of God, bind her heart close to you."

DIARMUID O'LAOGHAIRE

2 September

We are told always to keep a just attitude towards the rich, and we try. But as I thought of our breakfast line, our crowded house with people sleeping on the floor, when I thought of cold tenement apartments around us, and the lean gaunt faces of the men who came to us for help, desperation in their eyes, it was impossible not to hate, with a hearty hatred and a strong anger, the injustices of this world...

If Mary had appeared in Bethlehem clothed, as St John says, with the sun, a crown of twelve stars on her head, and the moon under her feet, then people would have fought to make way for her. But that was not God's way for her, nor is it Christ's way for Himself, now when he is disguised under every type of humanity that treads the earth.

DOROTHY DAY

3 September

Gifted beyond all that can be thought of or desired,
Black women were in the mind of the Lord
When He chose Mary.

(SOURCE UNKNOWN)

4 September

One of the two most powerful symbols of the Christian religion
is of a baby in its mother's arms – Jesus in the arms of Mary.
Always the sense is of peace, contentment, feminine grace and
gentleness, with soft, pleasing colours – blue, green, a deep red.
Often there is a sense of timelessness or eternity...In a world of
extraordinary brutality, here, in the very heart of Christianity, is
an image speaking to us of tenderness, of gentleness, of safety,
and of mutual loving...

But Mary plays an ambiguous role within Catholicism, not
part of the Godhead, yet sometimes revered more than any of
the persons of the Trinity. In a tiny village church in the Pyrenees
I remember a medieval statue in which Mary sits with the infant
Jesus on her lap. In His hands Jesus holds the book of the living
and the dead, the book that decides who shall be saved and
damned, but His mother holds her hands over His, making it
impossible for Him to open the book. Mary is 'soft-hearted',
apparently more merciful than God.

MONICA FURLONG

5 September

In flawless Oxbridge tones he [Father Bede Griffiths] proceeded
to speak for an hour...then turned to a personal experience that
recently shattered his own personal understanding. Seated outside his ashram hut one morning before dawn, Bede told us, he
was suddenly knocked to the ground by an invisible force during

meditation. Frightened, he managed to crawl to his bed, where he remained for a week in a semi-conscious state, attended by doctors unable to diagnose his condition. After ten days, the doctors were beginning to give up hope. Last rites were administered. Then one afternoon when Bede lay there dying, a voice came to him, whispering the following words: "Remember the Mother."…"It is the Mother," Bede went on to say, "who is the source of creation, and whose force is now being loosed upon the world. It is the Mother whose grace is so sorely needed by the Church, to help it enfold a suffering world, to quiet its fundamentalism, dissolve its bureaucracies, and heal this ailing planet."

BEDE GRIFFITHS,
QUOTED BY ANDREW HARVEY AND MARK MATOUSEK

6 September

Mary, Mater Dolorosa,
Walk me through the gloom.
Mary, Mentor of defiance,
Teach me your strength.
Mary, happy Queen of heaven:
The poor raised up!
Lady of final victory,
The hungry fed!
Symbol of beauty before me,
Increase my faith.

PETER DAINO

7 September

Holding her child, this peasant girl of Galilee will change and grow. She will hold him in countless attitudes, be clothed with countless forms of dress. She will become a lady of Byzantium or of Renaissance Italy, a Chinese princess, a woman of the African veldt. Yet however she is changed, she will forever contrive to do what she is doing in this cave. Forever her arms will encompass the child, forever give him birth, forever nourish him. She is more than Demeter, the great Earth Mother. Mary is 'Theotokos', the Mother of God, and Jesus, her child, is first among the sons of the morning.

HERBERT O'DRISCOLL

8 September

On the feast day of Mary the fragrant
Mother of the Shepherd of the flocks,
I cut me a handful of the new corn,
I dried it gently in the sun,
I rubbed it sharply from the husk
With mine own palms.

I ground it in a quern on Friday,
I baked it on a pan of sheepskin,
I toasted it to a fire of rowan,
And I shared it round my people.

I went sun-ways round my dwelling,
In name of Mary Mother,
Who promised to preserve me,
And who will preserve me,
In peace, in flocks,
In righteousness of heart.

GAELIC PRAYER

9 September

Because God has set aside His power, this woman of earth must now empower the child God has become.

HERBERT O'DRISCOLL

10 September

Parent of virtue, Light eternal, thou
Of whom was born the meek, benignant fruit,
That suffered on the Cross a bitter death
To save us sinners from the dark abyss,
Thou, Queen of Heaven, supreme and of this world,
Vouchsafe to entreat thy meritorious Son,
To lead me to His heavenly kingdom's joys
Through guidance of His never-failing grace.
Thou knowest my hope was ever placed in thee,
In thee, thou knowest, was still my sole delight;
O Goodness infinite, assist me now,
Help me, for at the bourne I am arrived,
Which I must soon inevitably pass;
My Comforter, Oh now desert me not,
For every fault committed here on earth
My soul deplores, and contrite is my heart.

DANTE ALIGHIERI

11 September

If we set ourselves to listen more to the faith of simple people in their relationship with Mary, which expresses their need for survival and for a fuller life, we will understand much better that theology has to be poetry, helping us to live more richly, and that it has to be prophecy, denouncing all forms of religious pharisaism and every kind of injustice. Theology is finally a Magnificat sung by women in the name of all the poor of the land who need bread, justice, liberty, and love.

IVONE GABARA

12 September

Mary is ever woman. The New Testament does not record her as divine. She stands with sinners beneath the Cross as the representative not of the Kingdom of God but of the Church on earth. The words of Christ in the Johannine Passion, "Woman, behold thy son," legitimately allow us to think of Mary as the Mother of the Christian family, the Church, the Church which is left on earth to be the community of the Holy Spirit and a home for all humanity.

GORDON WAKEFIELD

13 September

See, I have climbed the mountain side
Up to this holy house of God,
Where once that Angel-Painter trod
Who saw the heavens open wide,

And throned upon the crescent moon
The virginal white Queen of Grace –
Mary! Could I but see thy face,
Death could not come at all too soon.

O crowned by God with love and flame!
O crowned by Christ the Holy One!
O listen ere the searching sun
Show to the world my sin and shame.

OSCAR WILDE

14 September

Dear Mary, thou didst see thy first-born Son
Go forth to die amidst the scorn of men, for whom He died.
Receive my first-born son into thy arms

And keep him by thee till I come for him.
I have shared thy sorrow,
And soon shall share thy joy.

PADRAIC PEARSE

15 September

O Mother, O Mother,
Here is your hope, your joy, your pride,
Staggering up a leprous world to meet you.
Here is your flesh, your blood, your opened womb,
Here is your milk, your tears, your sleepless nights,
Here is your skin, the pulse you felt beneath your hand,
Here are your eyes, your colour, and the unmistakable smell.
Here are your dreams of feasting at a wedding.
Here is your youthful passion and your dancing days.
Here is your first fleshly imprint and your better self.
Here is your Child,
Staggering up a leprous road to meet you.

KATHY GALLOWAY

16 September

Let not my titles, crowns, and worldly honours
Cause me to glory in my rank and beauty.
Emperors are thy servants, as are kings.
I am a queen myself, and thy handmaiden –
All who would honour me should call me so.
O let my only glory be thy service.
Thou art the Queen of the Eternal Light.
We mortals reign, but over dreams and shadows.

MARIA DE MEDICI

17 September

Mary is today, as yesterday, not only present in the individual struggles of each person, but is involved in the collective struggles for liberation in Latin America. She is with all those who need land to live on, with those who campaign for better living conditions all round. Mary is an ally in the various campaigns for liberation, and, in this sense, she is more than a model for women to imitate. She is the symbol or, rather, one of the symbols of the energy of a people in search of economic, cultural, and religious autonomy. That is why, in the popular songs, she is called 'mother of the oppressed', 'ally of her people', 'liberator of us all'.

IVONE GEBARA

18 September

I received my first nurture in the faith from a woman. A woman taught me my first prayers. Woman for me was the natural eucharistic minister who held the family together, nourished it with love, moderated its disputes, turned its vexations into a Christian agape. Why should I, now or ever, decline to hear from a woman's lips the Word of God, or receive from her hands the bread of life? Who, I ask myself, has the power or the right to deny her these functions, which have been hers from the beginning?

MORRIS WEST

19 September

Did the woman say, as she held him for the first time,
In the dark of the stable,
After the pain, the bleeding, and the crying,
This is my Body, this is my Blood?

Did the woman say, as she held him for the last time,
In the dark of the garden,
After the pain, the bleeding, and the dying,
This is my Body, this is my Blood?

Well that she said it for him then,
For dried old men,
Brocaded robes belying barrenness,
Ordain that she not say it for him now.

ANON.

20 September

Perhaps it is no wonder that the women were first at the cradle
and last at the cross. They had never known a man like this
man – a prophet and teacher who never nagged at them, never
flattered or coaxed or patronised, who never made cruel jokes
about them, nor treated them either as 'The women, God help
us!' or 'The ladies, God bless them', who rebuked without queru-
lousness and praised without condescension, who took their
questions and arguments seriously; who never mapped out their
sphere for them, never urged them to be feminine or jeered at
them for being female; who had no axe to grind and no uneasy
male dignity to defend, who took them as he found them and was
completely unselfconscious.

DOROTHY SAYERS

21 September

There is not a single instance in the Gospels where Jesus cast
away a woman, as He did Herod Antipas, or cursed them as He
did the Scribes and Pharisees. To women He was merciful, wel-
coming, and affectionate, and He praised their faith and love.

The time has come for the Church to accept that her composi-
tion includes a feminine component, and to open to women all of
her ministries. After all, half the human race are women. And
the other half are the sons of women.

FREI BETTO

22 September

Woman is the companion of man, gifted with equal mental
capacities. She has the right to participate in every minutest
detail in the activities of man, and she has an equal right of freedom and liberty with him. By sheer force of vicious custom even
the most ignorant and worthless men have been enjoying a
superiority over women which they do not deserve and ought not
to have.

GANDHI

23 September

I have repeated times without number that non-violence is the
inherent quality of women. For ages men had the training in violence. In order to become non-violent, they have to cultivate the
qualities of women. Ever since I have taken to non-violence, I
have become more and more of a woman.

GANDHI

24 September

It moves one's heart to think:
Nine months before I was born
There was a woman who loved me deeply;
She did not know what I was going to be like,
But she loved me because she carried me in her womb.
And when she gave me birth,
She took me in her arms
Because her love was not just beginning –
She conceived it along with me.

OSCAR ROMERO

25 September

After a mother has smiled for a long time at her child, the child
will begin to smile back; she has awakened love in its heart, and
in awakening love in its heart she has awakened recognition.

HANS URS VON BALTHASAR

26 September

And when my mother, pretty as a church,
Takes me upon her lap, I laugh with love.

THOMAS MERTON

27 September

As a white candle
In a holy place,
So is the beauty
Of an aged face.

As the spent radiance
Of the winter sun,
So is a woman
With her travail done,

Her brood gone from her,
And her thoughts as still
As the waters
Under a ruined mill.

JOSEPH CAMPBELL

28 September

I remember thee in this solemn hour, my dear mother. I remember the days when thou didst dwell on earth and thy tender love watched over me like a guardian angel. Thou hast gone from me, but the bond which unites our souls can never be severed. Thine image lives within my heart. May the merciful Father reward thee for the faithfulness and kindness thou hast ever shown to me. May He lift up the light of His countenance upon thee and grant thee peace. Amen.

(SOURCE UNKNOWN)

29 September

Three friends go sightseeing. "Frisking neglected churches" they discover with help from each other, a fresco faded and luminous:

Sword-bearing Michael holding the terrible scales
Before the judgment seat from which her Son
Displays his pale pierced palms to a guilty world;
On one side, in the balance, naked, kneeling,
Hands hiding the sight from his eyes, a mannikin soul in
    hopeless case,
With the Devil himself pulling the scales awry with a secret
    finger,
The other side – look! Our Lady shines,
She's broken the thong of her necklace and is feeding the beads
Through her fingers into the other scale.

GUY BUTLER

30 September

The earth is at the same time Mother. She is Mother of all, for contained in her are the seeds of all. The earth of humankind contains all moistness, all verdancy, all germinating power. It is in so many ways fruitful. Yet it forms not only the basic raw material for humankind but also the substance of God's Son.

HILDEGAARD OF BINGEN

October

The Grace of Praying

1 October

We realize that we are going to have to create a new language of prayer. And this new language of prayer has to come out of something which transcends all our traditions, and comes out of the immediacy of love, the love that unites us in spite of real differences, real emotional friction...The things that are on the surface are nothing, what is deep is the real. We are creatures of love.

THOMAS MERTON

2 October

On the way to the mosque, O Lord, I passed the magyar in front of his flame, deep in thought. A little further on I heard a rabbi reciting his holy book in the synagogue. Then I came upon the church where the hymns sang gently in my ears. Finally I came to the mosque and watched the worshippers immersed in their experience. And I pondered upon how many are the different ways to You, the one God.

A SUFI MYSTIC

3 October

The humble, meek, merciful, just, pious, and devout souls are everywhere of one religion, and when death has taken off the mask, they will know one another, though the diverse liveries they wear here make them strangers.

WILLIAM PENN

4 October

Worship the light, not the lamp.
The lamps are different, the light is the same.
It comes from the Beyond.

                                                              RUMI

5 October

It seems that today, increasingly, the light is breaking through
unexpected cracks and apertures, through women and men of
varying and often contrasting cultural and religious backgrounds.
Christianity is not the sole transmitter of this light, yet nothing
contradicts, because at the centre all speak of the same divine
reality, some more purely than others, for much depends upon
the discipline and the purity of the human vessel through whom
these truths are transmitted.

                                            JAMES ROOSE-EVANS

6 October

Every day at exactly the same spots I pass men coming back from
the mosque. Most are old. Their walk, and a little breeze in their
long full clothes, give them a majestic air. We come up to each
other and exchange greetings:
    "May God receive your prayer."
    "May your day pass in peace."
    "May God come to your help."
    This morning ritual is more than a habit. It has become a
necessity. It prolongs their prayer at the mosque, and leads into
my Eucharist. The psalm goes on...

                                                         CATHERINE

7 October

Though the mystical theologies of the East and West differ widely, though the ideal of life they hold out to the soul differs too, yet in the experience of the saint this conflict is seen to be transcended. Where the love of God is reached, divergencies become impossible, for the soul has passed beyond the sphere of the manifold and is immersed in one reality. One cannot honestly say there is any wide difference between the Brahmin, the Sufi, or the Christian mystics at their best.

EVELYN UNDERHILL

8 October

Thou hast sent various prophets and teachers in various ages to various people…Thou art He that appears to be variously sought by various rites and art named by various names, since in Thy true being Thou remainest unknown and ineffable to all.

NICHOLAS OF CUSA

9 October

My dear friends, I draw no conclusions, much less do I want to give you advice. Dialogue is an ongoing process. We learn, we correct ourselves on our common march until we reach a state when both groups, Christians and Hindus, begin to accept each other as friends, brethren, and co-pilgrims on our way to the one and same goal – Brahman.

ISWAR PRASAD

10 October

Every form of prayer that is stirred by the Spirit, therefore, is in essence a repetition of the love word *Abba*, the Jesus word. It should be to the Christian what the syllable OM is to the Hindu, to be uttered not as the exclusive talisman of one religion, but as the password of humanity, establishing in Christ the ultimate truth of every human being.

JOHN TAYLOR

11 October

When I was a student, our family lived in a seaside town in the north of Sri Lanka. It was almost entirely a Hindu town. We were one of the only two Protestant families. As children, we played with the Hindu children, went to school with them, and in keeping with the practice in Asia we were in and out of one another's homes at all times of the day. In fact our next-door Hindu neighbours' two children regularly joined us in our evening family prayers. The prayers were elaborate affairs in those days, with singing of lyrics and choruses, Bible reading, and two or three persons, including children, offering the petitions. The Hindu children loved it and our neighbours were happy that their children joined us for prayers. Often some of us would be at our neighbours' when they had their *pujas* (Hindu prayers) and sang their *tevarams* (devotional songs). They extended warm and loving friendship to us. Long before I learned theology and was able to articulate religious matters, I had come to think of them as a family rooted in God's love.

WESLEY ARIARAJAH

12 October

You, the One
From Whom on different paths all of us have come,
To Whom on different paths all of us are going,
Make strong in our hearts what unites us.
Build bridges across all that divides us.
United make us rejoice in our diversity,
At one in our witness to your peace,
A rainbow of your glory.
Amen.

DAVID STEINDL-RAST

13 October

Send down, O God, O gentle and compassionate One, into my heart faith, tranquillity, and stillness, that I may be one of those whose hearts are made tranquil by the mention of God.

IBN-AL-ARABI

14 October

O God our Father, grant us that openness of heart and mind which will enable us to respect the personality, the customs, the beliefs, the opinions of others, however strange they may be to us. Grant that this openness may be grounded in confidence and trust, so that we may not, for fear, be forced to reject those who are different from ourselves.

JOHN PRICKETT

15 October

Prayer is perceiving the divine in noise and in quiet, in light and in dark, in the poetic and the mundane, in the play of children and in the faces of the old, in the laughter of the carefree and in the dull eyes of the poor or homeless, broken by life, work, or exposure.

STANISLAUS KENNEDY

16 October

Does God have a set way of prayer, that He expects each of us to follow? I doubt it. I believe some people – lots of people – pray through the witness of their lives, through the work they do, the friendships they have, the love they offer people and receive from people. Since when are words the only acceptable form of prayer?

DOROTHY DAY

17 October

Prayer is nothing else but a yearning of soul...When it is practised with the whole heart, it has great power. It makes a sour heart sweet, a sad heart merry, a poor heart rich, a foolish heart wise, a timid heart courageous, a sick heart well, a blind heart full of vision, a cold heart ardent. For it draws down the great God into the little heart; it drives the hungry soul up to the plenitude of God; it brings together these two lovers, God and the soul, in a wondrous place where they speak much of love.

MACHTHILD OF MAGDEBURG

18 October

Jesus assures us that many people will inherit the Kingdom (even though they will not think themselves entitled to do so) because they fed the hungry, gave drink to the thirsty, took in strangers, visited the sick and those in prison. Each of them has been proved to have true faith, and is beyond the need to recite any particular form of words.

Such a person has reached the climax of Christian life, as a result of which some Muslims may say of him or her, "He is a true Muslim," and Hindus, "She is faithful to the Karma," whilst Buddhists say, "He is a bodhsattva," and Jews "She is faithful to the House of Israel." Because such people, no matter what form of words they may use about their faith, are living embodiments of faith for all believers.

DONALD NICHOLL

19 October

As long as we imagine that the world can be changed by our activities, our good works, our energy, we substitute our effort for the power of God. That is as ineffective as it is blasphemous. "For Thine is the kingdom, the power ..." we pray, and then all too frequently behave as if His is the kingdom, and ours is the power – and the glory too! By contrast, if we see prayer as a means of releasing God's power into the world, of enabling Him to pour His transforming love into the critical centres of decision-making and activity, we begin to see paradoxically that we are not powerless at all. Our power to transform the world is God's power.

CHARLES ELLIOTT

20 October

Perhaps the prayer we make here may find its fulfilment on the
other side of the world. Perhaps the love we are given in a difficult moment came from a praying soul we never knew. It is all a
deep mystery, and we should be careful not to lay down hard and
fast rules.

EVELYN UNDERHILL

21 October

What the world is seeing in South Africa is a little goodness.
Goodness does prevail ultimately. This may seem like a slogan,
but the world is thrilled because the world ultimately warms to
goodness.

We have been prayed for, you know. This is a miracle. It is not
of our doing. We've been on the intercession list of the world for
a heck of a time. And it works. Yeh, man, it works!

DESMOND TUTU

22 October

The right relation between prayer and conduct is not that conduct is supremely important and prayer helps it, but that prayer
is supremely important and conduct is its test.

WILLIAM TEMPLE

23 October

It is actually astonishing that I can pray not just for myself but for
other people too, and that other people can pray not only for
themselves but for me as well. These intercessions bring us into a
great, often worldwide, fellowship of the Spirit. To know that this
fellowship is there, and intercedes for me when I fall silent, gives

me a powerful feeling of safe keeping...Life in the Spirit becomes a living life because people pray for one another and bring one another reciprocally to God.

JURGEN MOLTMANN

24 October

Lord of all creation, we stand in awe before you, impelled by visions of the harmony of humankind. We are children of many traditions, inheritors of shared wisdom and tragic misunderstandings, of proud hopes and humble successes. Now it is time for us to meet, in memory of truth, in courage and trust, in love and promise.

In the love which we share, let us see the common prayer of humanity.

In that in which we differ, let us wonder at the freedom of humankind.

In our unity and our differences, let us know the uniqueness that is God.

May our courage match our convictions, and our integrity match our hope.

May our faith in You bring us closer to one another.

May our meeting with past and present bring blessing for the future. Amen.

DANIEL FAIVRE

25 October

Jesus Christ, who reached across the ethnic boundaries between Samaritan, Roman, and Jew, who offered fresh sight to the blind and freedom to the captives, help us to break down the barriers in our community; enable us to see the reality of racism and bigotry, and free us to challenge and uproot them from ourselves, our society, and our world.

PRAYER LEAFLET FOR RACIAL JUSTICE

26 October

Lord, remind me when I am tempted to forget: You did not call me to defend your Church but to lay down my life for Your people.

COLIN WINTER

27 October

He lays no great burden upon us: a little remembrance of Him from time to time...To be with God, there is no need to be continually in church. We may make an oratory of the heart wherein to retire from time to time to converse with Him in humility, meekness, and love.

BROTHER LAWRENCE

28 October

I brought your tiredness home with me today and
held it in my arms awhile, touching it gently with my
love and hoping to embrace both it and you until
imagination blended into fact – and I was tired for you.

I brought your sadness home with me today and
circled it with tender strength, trying with loving
care to bind your soul with me until you knew
yourself at peace while I was sad *for* you.

Now that we meet again I cherish still these gifts of
yours that you had not given, and ask if I may keep
them close, drawing them deep into my love so that
my heart can share your pain – and I can ache *for you.*

ANN BIRD

29 October

Lord, I do not presume to tell you what to do or how or when to do it. I simply bring you people who need your love and whose needs your grace alone can meet. Let love reign, O Lord my God, let grace prevail.

PÈRE GROU

30 October

Generous God, you created this world for all to share.
Unclench our hands to let go of the greed which robs the poor.
Unclog our ears to hear the agony of all who cry for justice.
Unbind our hearts to recognize those who are oppressed by debt.
Open our lips to proclaim jubilee in our own time and place.
May our care be thorough and our solidarity be active.
May this community be a sign of hope:
For now is the favourable time. Amen.

JUBILEE PRAYER

31 October

Prayers like gravel flung at the sky's window,
Hoping to attract the loved one's attention,
But without visible plaits to let down
For the believer to climb up.
To what purpose open the casement?
I would have refrained long since
But that peering once through my locked fingers
I thought that I detected the movement of a curtain.

R. S. THOMAS

November

The Grace of Dying

1 November

At birth a child comes forth amid pain and danger from the narrow dwelling of the mother's womb into the broad light of day. In a similar way a man goes through the narrow gate of death when he departs this life. And though heaven and earth under which we now live appear so wide, so vast, yet in comparison with the heaven that shall be, it is far narrower and much smaller than is the womb in comparison with the broad expanse of heaven. That is why the death of saints is called a new birth, and their festivals birthdays.

MARTIN LUTHER

2 November

Faith's understanding of death is of a homecoming and a great banquet, of lovers meeting and walking together, of a joyous exploration of the infinite mystery of love. Faith reminds its children that in death they are renewed. So is all creation. Each petal from every rose that ever blossomed, each leaf from every larch that ever grew, each feather from every wren that ever nested, is received into heaven. Each smile from every child that ever played, each kiss from every mother that ever conceived, each tear from every man who ever cried, is renewed in heaven. Through the redemption won by Christ in the unlimited God of love may we, who are of no consequence, hope for a like glory.

DEREK WEBSTER

3 November

Death, be to me like a hand that shades my eyes,
Helping me to see into the light.

CHRISTOPHER FRY

4 November

There's something graceful about the dead,
And we who are left here
Fussing, eating,
Getting up and falling into bed.
There's something graceful about the dead,
And we who are left here,
With our tricks and lies,
We who are left here in the hurly-burly.
There's something graceful about the dead.
They died,
And are, all at once, dignified
As one who leaves a party early.

CHARLOTTE MITCHELL

5 November

The great gift, hidden in our dying, is the gift of unity with all people. However different we are, we are all born powerless, and the little differences we live in between dwindle in the light of this enormous truth... [W]e will make our passage to new life in solidarity with all the peoples of the earth.

I am deeply convinced that it is this joy, the joy of being the same as others, of belonging to the human family, that allows us to die well.

HENRI NOUWEN

6 November

As I walk this linear path I am aware of my own dying. My leaves are falling, seasons slip away. I am a pilgrim setting one foot before another on my own mortal journey. One foot before another, one step, another step, keep on walking, mindfully, gently, thankfully.

BROTHER RAMON

7 November

Death is the touchstone of our attitude to life. People who are afraid of death are afraid of life. It is impossible not to be afraid of life, with all its complexities and dangers, if one is afraid of death...It is only if we can face death, make sense of it, determine its place and our place in regard to it, that we will be able to live in a fearless way and to the fulness of our ability...If only we realized, whenever confronted with a person, that this might be the last moment of his life or ours, we would be much more intense, much more attentive to the words we speak and the things we do. Only awareness of death will give life this immediacy and depth, will bring life to life.

ANTHONY OF SOUROZH

8 November

All overgrown by cunning moss,
All interspersed with weed,
The little cage of Currer Bell
In quiet Haworth land.

Gathered from many wanderings –
Gethsemane can tell
Thro' what transporting anguish
She reached the Asphodel.

Soft fall the sounds of Eden
Upon her puzzled ear.
Oh, what an afternoon for Heaven
When Brontë entered there!

EMILY DICKINSON

9 November

Winter is on my head, but eternal spring is in my heart. The nearer I approach the end, the plainer I hear around me the immortal symphonies of the worlds which invite me...For half a century I have been writing thoughts in prose, verse, history, drama, romance, tradition, satire, ode, and song. I have tried them all, but I feel I have not said a thousandth part of that which is within me. When I go down to the grave, I can say, I have finished my day's work, but I cannot say, I have finished my life's work.

VICTOR HUGO

10 November

As my own life reaches on toward its inevitable close, I feel more and more as if I am living in a tent. The sunshine of other days is bound, to a certain extent, to be muted, but more and more the canvas becomes transparent, as light begins to filter in from the other side. I seem more and more to be living at the junction of matter and spirit. In these latter days I can draw near to the writer of an old Scottish evangelical hymn, a woman who lived in my father's native Irvine and who sang her life's song of thankfulness and praise, using the homely image of cloth-making:

With mercy and with judgment my web of time He wove
And aye the dews of sorrow were lustred by His love.
I'll praise the hand that guided, I'll praise the heart that planned
Where glory, glory dwelleth in Immanuel's land.

MARGARET STANSGATE

11 November

When you are standing at your hero's grave,
Or near some homeless village where he died,
Remember, through your heart's rekindling pride,
The German soldiers who were loyal and brave.

Men fought like brutes, and hideous things were done;
And you have nourished hatred, harsh and blind.
But in that Golgotha perhaps you'll find
The mothers of the men who killed your son.

SIEGFRIED SASSOON

12 November

Set up no stone to keep alive my name.
I am content that when I have gone from earth
The few who shared my pathway for a while
And who so generously gave me love
All memory of me should be dispersed
And thinned to nothing by the winds of time.
Enough that in the timeless mind of God
I shall be held and loved eternally.

LOUIE HORNE

13 November

I must first say, quite decidedly, that the closing hours of a man's
life are no different from any others. I had always imagined that
one would have no feeling beyond shock and that one would keep
saying to oneself, "This is the last time you'll see the sun go down;
this is the last time you'll go to bed; you've only twice more to
hear the clock strike twelve." But there is no question of any of
that. Perhaps I'm a little above myself, I don't know, but I cannot

deny that I feel in the best of spirits at the moment...I am quite certain that you will never lose me on this earth, no, not for a moment. And this fact it was given us to symbolize finally through our common participation in the Holy Communion, that celebration which was my last. I wept for a little, not that I was sad, not that I was disquieted, not that I wanted to turn back – no, I wept for gratitude because I am overwhelmed by this proof of the existence of God. True, we cannot see Him face to face, but we cannot but be awestruck when we suddenly realize that a whole lifetime through He has gone before us as the cloud by day and the fire by night.

HELMUT VON MOLTKE

14 November

I remember finally a man who had come to terms with death, learned confidence in a loving God, and believed in and looked forward to Paradise. He was an old French Jesuit. When his last moments had come, a few scholastics were asked to pray by his bedside. As they stood there, suitably grave and recollected, the old man opened one eye and said in a weak voice, "Open the drawer at the foot of the cupboard." One of them did so and found a bottle of champagne and some glasses. "Fill up your glasses," the old man said. One of the scholastics did as he was told and they stood for a moment wondering what to do next. The old man opened up the other eye and said rather gruffly, "What about me?" So they gave him a glass. Then he said, "I've lived a very happy life. I'd like you to drink with me to a happy death." They drank the toast, and five minutes later he died. A good death; but then he had spent his life learning to love his enemies.

JOHN HARRIOTT

15 November

Death is but crossing the world, as friends do the seas; they live in one another still. For they must needs be present that love, and live in that which is omnipresent. This is the comfort of friends, that though they may be said to die, yet their friendship and society are ever present, because immortal.

WILLIAM PENN

16 November

I have got my leave.
Bid me farewell, my friends,
I bow to you and take my departure.

Here I give back the keys of my door,
and I give up all claim to my house.
I only ask for last kind words from you.

We were neighbours for long,
but I have received more than I could give.
Now the day has dawned,
and the lamp that lit my dark corner is out.
A summons has come,
and I am ready for my journey.

RABINDRANATH TAGORE

17 November

There is a place called City-of-no-Sorrows,
There is no grieving and no suffering there,
No taxman, no tribute, no levies,
No worrying, no sin, no fear, no death.
Wonderful country for my home, my friend,
Where all is good and everyone happy.

In the Eternal Kingdom of my Lord
No rich or poor, all are equal.
Full of people, a famous place
Of the wise and prosperous.
They enjoy their walks as they please.
No palace guards or police restrict them.
Ravidas, the emancipated cobbler says,
My fellow citizen, is my friend.

RAVIDAS

18 November

There is a ripeness oftime for death, regarding others as well as
ourselves, when it is reasonable we should drop off and make way
for another growth. When we have lived our generation, we
should not wish to encroach on another.

THOMAS JEFFERSON

19 November

When a good person dies, darkness descends on us. We feel lost,
bereft, forlorn. But gradually the lights begin to come on, as we
recall the good deeds done by the deceased. They spring up all
over the place. We are amazed at how much light is generated. In
this strange and beautiful light we not only find our way, but find
the meaning of life itself.

FLOR McCARTHY

20 November

The tissue of the life to be
We weave with colours all our own,
And in the field of Destiny
We reap as we have sown.

JOHN GREENLEAF WHITTIER

21 November

We send our brother [Cesara Chevaz] to God's vineyards with the words of Chicano playwright, Luis Valdez: "Cesar, we plant your heart, like a seed. You shall never die. The seed of your heart will keep on singing, keep on flowering, for the cause. All farmworkers shall harvest in the seed of your memory. And so shall the rest of us too."

AARON GALLEGOS AND ROSE MARIE BERGER

22 November

In September I lost a precious friend after a three year battle with cancer. In her final months, as she courageously continued to reach out to others with her love, concern, and prayers, Maureen found enduring strength in the words, "Jesus carries me." She did not say to her family and friends, "I carry Jesus in my mind and heart." In her loneliness and pain she touched the heart of the matter with the mantra she shared, "Jesus carries me."

GERALD O'COLLINS

23 November

Nel and Sula did not touch hands or look at each other during the funeral. There was a space, a separateness, between them ...Then they left their pews. For with some emotions one has to stand. They spoke, for they were full and needed to say. They swayed, for the rivulets of grief or of ecstasy must be rocked. And when they thought of all that life and death locked into that little closed coffin, they danced and screamed, not to protest God's will but to acknowledge it and confirm once more their conviction that the only way to avoid the Hand of God is to get into it.

TONI MORRISON

24 November

Our friends go with us as we go
Along the path, where Beauty wends,
Where all we love foregathers: so
Why should we fear to join our friends?

Who would survive them to outlast
His children, to outwear his fame –
Left when the Triumph has gone past –
To win from Age not Time a name?

Then do not shudder at the knife
That Death's indifferent hand drives home,
But with the strivers leave the strife
Nor, after Caesar, skulk in Rome.

                                    OLIVER GOGARTY

25 November

After a consultant had said to me on Monday that he wouldn't be
needing to see me any more, I could just go home, and so on,
there came into my mind the thought – well, now my sails are set
for the journey home. And I remembered Jesus's words to His
disciples when He said, "I go to prepare a place for you." And
that's what going home means, you go to the place that is prepared for you. And I am also hoping that, in some measure, if
you are a follower of Jesus, you can also do something which He
does, that is to say, prepare a place for one's loved ones who are
going to follow after. Going home means also preparing a place
for you to come when your time arrives...

    The last word is not with corruption and death and nothing-
ness, but with love, just as the first word of creation is love. If we
have that faith, we can then trust ourselves with our bodies and
our spirits to the universe, to the centre of the universe, to the
heart of the universe.

                                    DONALD NICHOLL

26 November

He was a five year old Iraqi boy, dying of leukaemia. I stroked his puffy little face, and his tiny hand grabbed mine and squeezed. I knew then that it was possible to die of shame.

FELICITY ARBUTHNOT

27 November

James was too weak to hold his granddaughter Hazel in his arms. So on returning from the church after the christening the family lifted her up in front of the dying man. And he said, "Hazel, you are the joy of my life, and the end of my rainbow." He died a few days later.

DONAL O'DOHERTY

28 November

On the day when death will knock at your door,
What will you offer him?

Oh, I will set before my guest
The full vessel of my life,
I will never let him go with empty hands.

All the sweet vintage
Of all my autumn days and summer nights,
All the earnings and gleanings of my busy life
Will I place before him
At the close of my days
When death will knock at my door.

RABINDRANATH TAGORE

29 November

I am no longer afraid of death,
I know well
its dark, cold corridors
leading to life.

I am afraid rather of that life
which does not come out of death,
which cramps our hands
and slows our march.

I am afraid of my fear
and even more of the fear of others,
who do not know where they are going,
who continue clinging
to what they think is life
which we know to be death!

I live each day to kill death;
I die each day to give birth to life,
and in this death of death,
I die a thousand times
and am reborn a thousand times
through that love
from my People
which nourishes hope!

JULIA ESQUIVEL

30 November

I think that the dying pray at the last, not please but thank you,
as a guest thanks the host at the door.

ANNIE DILLARD

December

The Grace of Waiting

1 December

Grace doesn't keep. It is given for now, not for cold storage. Look back on your life – you always received the grace of the moment, but never a future instalment.

DONAGH O'SHEA

2 December

The ultimate reason for our hope is not to be found at all in what we want, wish, and wait for; the ultimate reason is that we are wanted and wished and waited for. We are waited for as the prodigal son is waited for by his father. We are accepted and received as a mother takes her children into her arms and comforts them. God is our last hope because we are God's last love.

JURGEN MOLTMANN

3 December

Our waiting is meant to be active, highly sensitized to whatever may happen in an apparently empty time. We are looking in the darkness for changes, signs of the new world to come, and we are listening in the silence for a voice. It is not always loud, as it was for Saul when it knocked him off his horse, but it can be astonishingly peremptory. It has sometimes made me get up from my desk and rush half a mile to the nearest church, simply to put myself before the Sacrament. And perhaps what happens in these rare, strange cases is not that we suddenly can't wait for God, but that God – who not only has all time, but is all time – suddenly can't wait for us.

ANN WROE

4 December

My Lord, where I have offended
Do thou forgive it me,
That so, when all being ended
I hear Thy last decree,
I may go up to Jerusalem
Out of Galilee.

JOHN MEADE FALKNER

5 December

He will come like last leaf's fall,
one night when the November wind
has flayed the trees to bone, and earth
wakes choking on the mould,
the soft shroud's folding.

He will come like frost,
one morning when the shrinking earth
opens on mist, to find itself
arrested in the net
of alien, sword-set beauty.

He will come like dark,
one evening when the bursting red
December sun draws up the sheet
and penny-masks its eye to yield
the star-snowed fields of sky.

He will come, will come,
will come like crying in the night,
like blood, like breaking,
as the earth writhes to toss him free.
He will come like child.

ROWAN WILLIAMS

6 December

To skim your eyes watching the skies for the return of Christ is as misguided as to wait for archeologists to dig up evidence for the fall of Adam. For both are ways of trying to make vivid what Christians believe is true not just of one moment but of every moment. Everywhere, at any moment, Christ comes in. That is what the doctrine of the Second Coming is concerned to assert. The trouble about the phrase 'the second coming' is that it suggests that Christ is coming again only once...but in fact you won't find the phrase in the Bible. It speaks simply of 'the coming of Christ' and the word it uses means 'presence'...It's that man again...The New Testament writers couldn't describe even the most secular, political events without seeing Christ meeting and judging human beings in them.

JOHN ROBINSON

7 December

Life can be understood only backwards, but it must be lived forwards.

SØREN KIERKEGAARD

8 December

I am convinced it is a great art to know how to grow old gracefully and I am determined to practise it...I always thought I should love to grow old, and I find it is even more delightful than I thought. It is so delicious to be done with things, and to feel no need any longer to concern myself much about earthly affairs... I am tremendously content to let one activity after another go, and to await quietly and happily the opening of the door at the end of the passageway that will let me in to my real abiding place.

HANNAH WHITALL PEARSALL SMITH

9 December

In our old age, with diminishing physical and mental powers, our heart can still long for and pray for the well-being of all peoples. Perhaps those prayers, wrung from us in our weakness and help-lessness, we will one day discover to have been the most effective moments of our lives, preparing us for the next stage of our jour-ney, when we can more effectively work for the salvation of all peoples and all creation.

GERARD HUGHES

10 December

Our good Sister seems to me full of good will, but she wants to go faster than grace. One does not become holy all at once.

BROTHER LAWRENCE

11 December

You must never get it into your head that you have arrived at a certain state...We shall be all the more rich the more we think ourselves poor. Every day you must say to yourself, Today I am going to begin.

JEAN PIERRE DE CAUSSADE

12 December

A disciple asked the Holy One, "Where shall I look for enlight-enment?"
    "Here," the Holy One said.
    "When will it happen?"
    "It is happening right now," the Holy One said.
    "Then why don't I experience it?"
    "Because you do not look," the Holy One said.
    "What should I look for?"

"Nothing," the Holy One said. "Just look."

"At what?"

"Anything your eyes light upon," the Holy One said.

"Must I look in a special way?"

"No," the Holy One said. "The ordinary way will do."

"But don't I always look the ordinary way?"

"No," the Holy One said. "You don't."

"Why ever not?" the disciple demanded.

"Because to look you must be here," the Holy One said.

"You're mostly somewhere else."

JOAN CHITTISTER

13 December

It is in this way that the Church can become what Pope John XXIII called the village fountain…It can become a place where the people of the village can stop by for clean water, for water that comes from afar, and brings with it tastes, echoes, tensions, and passions of distant worlds. The village fountain is perhaps, as in some Byzantine places, the holy fountain where one can buy images of the mother of God, and where all come, the citizens, the sick, the rich and poor alike, pilgrims and traders to be cured of their diseases, of their closures and their egoisms…We in the Community of Sant' Egidio like to be in harmony with this village fountain and we are content to be able to spend ourselves for this end.

MARIO MARAZZITI

14 December

A poor man is one who has to sit and wait, and wait, and wait, in clinics, in offices, in places where you sign papers, in police stations, etc. And he has nothing to say about it.

THOMAS MERTON

15 December

Love is not commensurate with time. Think for example of someone you have loved who is now dead. And imagine that a higher being says to you, "I can guarantee that you will see your beloved again, but you will have to wait 30,000 years." Will you wait? Anyone who knows love will unhesitatingly say Yes. "Will you wait a million years?" Again the answer is Yes. Love has no end.

DONALD NICHOLL

16 December

In the end, the vista of future loneliness allows only a choice between two alternatives: either to despair in desolation or to stake so high on the possibility that one acquires the right to life in a communion beyond the individual. But doesn't choosing the second call for the kind of faith which moves mountains?

DAG HAMMARSKØLD

17 December

There is only one test of our prayer life. Are we wanting God? Do we want Him so much that we'll go on if it takes five, six, ten years to find Him? With that steady determination that even goes on when there seems no access at all? The primary object of prayer is to know God better; we and our needs should come second.

FLORENCE ALLSHORN

18 December

Go down into the plans of God, go down deep as you may. Fear not for your fragility under that weight of water. Fear not the power of treacherous currents under the sea. Simply, do not be afraid. Let go. You will be led like a child whose mother holds him to her bosom and against all comers is his shelter.

HELDER CAMARA

19 December

You're waiting in Islamabad,
And waiting in Delhi,
You're waiting out in Bangladesh,
Waiting there for me:
I'm waiting here in Manchester,
Waiting and hoping too,
Trying to preserve my dignity
Whilst waiting here for you.

PAUL WELLER

20 December

The African continent knows poverty and death by name, but we are not a dying continent because we refuse to give up. We refuse to give up on God, we refuse to give up on ourselves, and we refuse to give up on the churches. Every day is a jubilee in Africa, because the jubilee for the downtrodden is about the love of God that proclaims mercy to the condemned. A continent that knows how brief life can be cannot afford to invest in fifty years of waiting. Rather, the spirituality of not giving up invites everyone to live today as if tomorrow will not come. Turn to God today and rejoice in hope, for tomorrow may never be.

MUSIMBI KANYORO

21 December

Since spring she has contained the world
And time and all we know of it,
For she bears God, a human child
To save us all and make us fit
A scheme that makes the beggar bold,
For this the stars are candles lit.

To shine in Bethlehem once more
As every year but always new,
A maiden holds a God in store
At whose sweet birth the angels bow.
Christmas is what the world waits for
When past and future meet in NOW.

ELIZABETH JENNINGS

22 December

We found no star or stable, no pious ox or ass
though there were engaging pigs, bred for roasting,
trivialized in Manila's Christmas tinsel.
Here the solemnity of Christ's coming
set the stark earth aglow.
Mary's strong daughters cradled human dignity,
ready to defend land or freedom,
weaving a pattern of justice.
Their mothers' love confronted exploitation's lust
and touched the hills with glory.

MICHAEL HARE DUKE

23 December

Don't hide, don't run, but rather discover in the midst of life a new way forward: a Christmas journey sometimes marked by fragility and tears; and on that road to hold these hands that even in their brokenness create a new tomorrow.

PETER MILLAR

24 December

This was the moment when Before
Turned into After, and the future's
Uninvented timekeepers presented arms.

This was the moment when nothing
Happened. Only dull peace
Sprawled boringly over the earth.
This was the moment when even energetic Romans
Could find nothing better to do
Than counting heads in remote provinces.

And this was the moment
When a few farm workers and three
members of an obscure Persian sect

Walked haphazardly by starlight straight
Into the Kingdom of heaven.

U. A. FANTHORPE

25 December

And the Word became flesh and dwelt among us, and we beheld His glory, the glory as of the only begotten of the Father, full of grace and truth.

GOSPEL ACCORDING TO JOHN

26 December

Mary…Mary astonished by God,
on a straw bed circled by beasts,
and an astonished old husband, Mary marinka,
holy woman, split by sanctified seed
into mother and father forever,
we pray for you, sister and woman,
shook by the awe-full affection of the saints.

LUCILLE CLIFTON

27 December

Holy Child of Bethlehem,
whose parents found no room in the inn,
we pray for all who are homeless…

Holy Child of Bethlehem,
rejected stranger,
we pray for all who are lost, alone,
all who cry for loved ones…

Holy Child of Bethlehem,
in you the Eternal was pleased to dwell;
help us, we pray, to see the divine image
in people everywhere.

DAVID BLANCHFLOWER

28 December

And it came to pass when the Lord Jesus was born at Bethlehem
of Judea, in the time of King Herod, behold, Magi came from
the East to Jerusalem as Zarathustra (Zoroaster) had predicted;
and there were with them gifts, gold, and frankincense, and

myrrh. And they adored Him, and presented to Him their gifts. Then the Lady Mary took one of the swaddling bands, and on account of the smallness of her means, gave it to them, and they received it from her with the greatest marks of honour. And in the same hour there appeared to them an angel in the form of a star, which had before guided them on their journey; and they went away following the guidance of its light, until they arrived in their own country.

FROM AN ARABIC GOSPEL

29 December

And their kings and chief men came to them asking what they had seen or done, how they had gone and come back, what they had brought with them. And they showed them that cloth which the Lady Mary had given them. Wherefore they celebrated a feast, and according to their custom, lighted a fire and worshipped it, and threw that swaddling cloth into it, and the fire laid hold of it and enveloped it. And when the fire had gone out, they took out the swaddling cloth, exactly as it had been before, just as if the fire had not touched it. Wherefore they began to kiss it, and to put it on their heads and their eyes, saying, "This verily is the truth without doubt. Assuredly it is a great thing that the fire was not able to burn or destroy it." They took it, and with the greatest honour, laid it up among their treasures.

FROM AN ARABIC GOSPEL

30 December

Let us plant dates, even though those who plant them will never eat them. We must live by the love of what we will never see. This is the secret discipline. It is a refusal to let the creative act be dissolved away in immediate sense experience, and a stubborn commitment to the future of our grandchildren. Such disciplined love is what has given prophets, revolutionaries, and saints the courage to die for the future they envisaged. They make their own bodies the seed of their brightest hope.

REUBEN ALVES

31 December

Wait till the end and you will see the outcome of events. Don't fuss, don't worry yet awhile. Imagine someone, born and bred on the sea, being suddenly landed on terra firma and not having the least notion about agriculture. He sees a farmer collecting grain and shutting it in a barn to protect it from damp. Then he sees this same farmer take the same grain and cast it to the winds, spreading it on the ground, maybe in the mud, without worrying any more about the dampness. Surely he will think that the farmer has ruined the grain, and he will reprove him.

Is such reproof justified? Yes, it is, not on grounds of fact but because of the ignorance of the judgment made. No it is not, because of the pride and rashness of the judgment made. Because, if this individual, before committing himself, had waited for the summer, he would have changed his ideas. He would have seen the corn waving in the fields, he would have seen the farmer sharpening his scythe to reap the very grain he had scattered and left to rot; he would have seen how greatly the grain had multiplied.

Now, if the farmer waits all winter, so much the more ought you to await the final outcome of events, remembering who it is who ploughs the soil of our souls.

JOHN CHRYSOSTOM

SOURCES AND ACKNOWLEDGEMENTS

The compilers and publisher have done their best to trace all copyright holders. They know they have not been completely successful, particularly with short quotations from Asian and Middle Eastern sources, for which omission this is a particular and general apology. With so many medium-sized publishers going out of business, with some imprints surviving but as subsidiaries of large international companies, and with the copyright laws now covering authors until seventy-five years after their deaths, the whole business of chasing permissions has become worryingly complicated and subject to increasing delays. There is much tearing of hair, and we can but hope that anyone who has been inadequately acknowledged will forgive us. The publisher would be grateful to be informed of any errors or omissions in the following acknowledgements

As Pauline Webb indicates in her Preface, busy people scribble on scraps of paper when they come across gems, and they are rarely academic researchers who scrupulously keep records of every conceivable detail. At the very least she and Nadir Dinshaw hope they have quoted and attributed accurately.

1 January	Dietrich Bonhoeffer, *Letters and Papers from Prison*, SCM Press, 1953, quoted by permission of SCM Press for the UK, and Simon Schuster for the USA
2 January	Paul Tillich, *The Shaking of the Foundations*, Penguin, 1962, and SCM Press
3 January	Sister Stanislaus Kennedy, *A Bundle of Blessings*, St Paul Publishers
4 January	Allen Birtwhistle, *Draw Near With Faith*, Epworth Press
5 January	Dionysius the Areopagite, Letter Eight to Demophilius
6 January	The Feast of the Epiphany, Evelyn Waugh, *Helena*, Chapman & Hall; rights with Random House; Helena was the mother of the Emperor Constantine
7 January	Abram Terts, quoted in Andrei Sinyavsky, *A Voice from the Chorus*, HarperCollins, 1976, quoted with permission
8 January	Fergal Keane, *Letter to Daniel*, Penguin, 1996, quoted with permission
9 January	George Basil, Cardinal Hume, *Basil in Blunderland*, Darton, Longman, & Todd, 1997, quoted with permission
10 January	Francis Thompson, quoted by Alice Meynell
11 January	Ben Okri, 'To an English friend in Africa', *An Africa Elegy*
12 January	Simone Weil, *An Anthology*, Virago Press, quoted with permission
13 January	Martin Luther, *Daily Readings with Martin Luther*, Darton, Longman, and Todd
14 January	Mataji Vandana, RSCJ
15 January	Dorothy Sayers, *Unpopular Opinions*, quoted with permission of David Higham Associates
16 January	Fritz Reuter, quoted by Dietrich Bonhoeffer
17 January	Martin Luther King Jnr, *Strength to Love*, Fontana, 1969, also USA 1963, renewed 1991, copyright Coretta Scott King and the heirs to the estate, quoted with permission
18 January	Colin Morris, *Mankind is my Church*, Hodder & Stoughton, 1971, quoted with permission of William Neill-Hall Ltd
19 January	Aung San Suu Kyi
20 January	Desmond Tutu, quoted with the permission of the author
21 January	Alan Jones, *Soul-Making*, SCM Press, 1986, and HarperCollins, quoted with permission
22 January	Ralph Waldo Emerson, 1885
23 January	Mother Teresa of Calcutta, as reported in *The Tablet*, quoted with permission
24 January	Robert Browning, 'Epistle from Karshish'
25 January	Feast of the Conversion of St Paul: St Paul, The First Letter to the Corinthians, 15.9–10, New Revised Standard Version of the Bible
26 January	Hubert Richards, *St Paul and his Epistles*, Darton, Longman, and Todd, 1979, quoted with permission
27 January	Rose Macaulay, *The Towers of Trebizond*

28 January	Rumi, Persian Sufi mystic
29 January	Iris Murdoch, *Nuns and Soldiers*, Chatto and Windus, 1980, quoted with permission of the Random House Group
30 January	Antony Bridge, *One Man's Advent*, Grafton Books, 1986
31 January	R. S. Thomas, *Later Poems*, Macmillan
1 February	Elizabeth Jennings, *Moments of Grace*, Carcanet Press, 1979, quoted with permission
2 February	Presentation of Christ in the Temple, Edward Schillebeeckx
3 February	Sir Ralph Turner MC who served with the Third Queen Alexandra's own Gurkha Rifles in the First World War
4 February	Louie Horne, 'A Light to Walk by', Quaker friend of Nadir Dinshaw by correspondence
5 February	Thomas Traherne
6 February	Kathleen Raine, 'A Nice Little World', George Allen & Unwin, with apologies for the incomplete reference
7 February	Robert Browning
8 February	Elizabeth Barratt Browning
9 February	John Ruskin
10 February	Thomas Merton, *Asian Journal (The Eastward Flight)*, 1973, New Directions Publishing Corporation
11 February	J. W. N. Sullivan, *But for the Grace of God*, Jonathan Cape, quoted with permission
12 February	Emily Dickinson
13 February	Ann Wroe, writing in *The Tablet*, quoted with permission
14 February	Sa'di, translated J. C. E. Bowen, *Poems from the Persian*, Faber and Faber
15 February	Sarah Orne Jewett
16 February	Monica Furlong, *Travelling In*, Hodder & Stoughton, 1975
17 February	Jean Claude Dietsch, quoted in Pedro Arrupe, *Itineraire d'un Jesuite*
18 February	Andrew Harvey and Mark Matousek, *Dialogues with a Modern Mystic*, Theosophical Publishing House, Illinois, quoted with permission
19 February	Denise Levertov, *Sands of the Well*, Bloodaxe, quoted with permission
20 February	W. B. Yeats
21 February	From the Sanskrit: apologies for incomplete reference
22 February	Vera Brittain, *Testament of Friendship*, Cedric Chivers Ltd, 1971
23 February	Daniel O'Leary, *Windows of Wonder*, Columba Press, 1991, quoted with permission
24 February	Dorothy Sayers, *The Zeal of Thy House*, 1961, quoted with permission from David Higham Associates
25 February	Siegfried Sassoon, *The War Poems*, Faber & Faber, 1983, by kind permission of George Sassoon
26 February	John Masefield, 'An Epilogue'
27 February	Colin Morris, *Raising the Dead*, 1996

28 February	C. F. Andrewes: apologies for incomplete reference
29 February	From the Sukhmani from the Sikh tradition
1 March	St David's Day. Rowan Williams, translating a poem by Waldo Williams, *After the Silent Centuries*, quoted with permission
2 March	Joan Fitch, *Handicap and Bereavement*, Friends' Fellowship of Healing, quoted with permission
3 March	Henri Nouwen, 'All is Grace', November/December 1992 issue of *Weavings*, quoted with permission
4 March	David Jenkins, *Freedom to Believe*, BBC Worldwide Ltd, 1991, quoted with permission
5 March	Michael Mayne, from a sermon quoted in *The Tablet*, quoted with permission
6 March	Ann Lewin, from 'Healing', Foundery Press, 1997, quoted with permission
7 March	John A. T. Robinson, quoted in Eric James, *A Life of Bishop John Robinson*, HarperCollins, 1987
8 March	Alan Ecclestone, *The Night Sky of the Lord*, Darton, Longman, and Todd, quoted with permission
9 March	Anonymous, found on a scrap of paper in a Nazi concentration camp
10 March	Elie Wiesel, *Night*, Penguin Books, 1958, original copyright Les Editions Minuit, quoted with permission
11 March	Helen Waddell, *Peter Abelard*, Constable and Robinson Publishing Ltd, quoted with permission
12 March	Bishop Michael Hare Duke: apologies for incomplete reference
13 March	Eric James, *A Time to Speak*, SPCK
14 March	Sheila Cassidy, *Good Friday People*, Darton, Londman, and Todd, quoted with permission
15 March	Dorothee Sölle: apologies for incomplete reference
16 March	Margaret Spufford, quoted in *Spiritual Classics of the Twentieth Century*
17 March	St Patrick's Day. Patrick of Ireland, *The Wisdom of the Saints*, OUP
18 March	Kenneth Leech, from an article in *The Independent*, 30 September 1989
19 March	St Joseph's Day. Tissa Balasuriya, *Mary and Human Liberation*, Mowbray, Continuum
20 March	Richard Holloway, *The Stranger in the Wings*, SPCK
21 March	Anonymous
22 March	Sa'di, op. cit., 14 February
23 March	Henri Nouwen, *Out of Solitude*, Ave Maria Press, quoted with permission
24 March	Aine Cox, from an article in *The Tablet*, quoted with permission
25 March	The Feast of the Annunciation. Mary Grey: apologies for incomplete reference

26 March	Leo Tolstoy, quoted by Johann Arnold, *I Tell You a Mystery*, Plough Publishing, quoted with permission
27 March	Johann Arnold, op. cit. 26 March
28 March	Sister Frances Dominica, in ed. Dan Cohn-Sherbok, *Tradition and Unity*, Bellew, 1991, quoted with permission
29 March	Edmund Banyard, 'Judgment', *Turn but a Stone*, National Christian Education Council, 1992, quoted by permission of the author
30 March	Rumi, Persian Sufi mystic
31 March	St Paul, The First Letter to the Corinthians 12.7–10, New Revised Standard Version of the Bible

1 April	John Wesley: apologies for incomplete reference
2 April	Thomas a Kempis, *The Imitation of Christ*
3 April	Francis of Assisi: apologies for incomplete reference
4 April	St Augustine of Hippo: apologies for incomplete reference
5 April	Richard Rolle: apologies for incomplete reference
6 April	Jeremy Taylor: apologies for incomplete reference
7 April	Buddhist Scriptures: Sutta Nipata I, 8
8 April	Percy Bysshe Shelley, *Defence of Poetry*
9 April	Leo Tolstoy, *Yasnaya Polyana*, Brown University Press
10 April	Epicurus, *c.* 300 BC
11 April	St Aelred of Rievaulx, *c.* 1150: apologies for incomplete reference
12 April	Martin Forward: apologies for incomplete reference
13 April	Kenneth Walker, *Introduction to Women Saints*, Vedanta Press
14 April	John O'Donohue, *Anam Cara, Spiritual Wisdom from the Celtic World*, Bantam Press, 1997
15 April	Vincent van Gogh, from a letter to his brother, Theo
16 April	Fyodr Dostoevsky, *The Brothers Karamazov*, translated © David Magashack, Penguin Classics, 1958, quoted with permission
17 April	Hrabanus Maurus, AD 776–856, To Grimold, Abbot of St Gall
18 April	Gandhi the Mahatma: apologies for incomplete reference
19 April	Robert Browning: apologies for incomplete reference
20 April	J. B. Priestley, quoted by Diana Collins, quoted by permission of Tom Priestley
21 April	C. Day Lewis,'Walking away', *The Gate*, 1962, reproduced in *The Complete Poems*, Sinclair Stevenson, 1992, quoted with permission of Random House Group
22 April	C. Day Lewis, 'My mother's sister', *The Room*, 1965, reproduced in *The Complete Poems*, Sinclair Stevenson, 1992, quoted with permission of Random House Group
23 April	William Shakespeare, Sonnet CXVI
24 April	Father Alexander Elchaninov: apologies for incomplete reference
25 April	Henri Nouwen, *The Inner Voice of Love*, Darton, Longman, and Todd, quoted with permission

26 April	Sister Claire M. Prevallet SL: apologies for incomplete reference
27 April	St Thérèse of Lisieux: apologies for incomplete reference
28 April	William Dalrymple, *From the Holy Mountain*, Flamingo, 1997, quoted with permission
29 April	Andrew Harvey and Mark Matousek, *Dialogues with a Modern Mystic*, Theosophical Publishing House, Illinois, quoted with permission
30 April	St Paul, The First Letter to the Corinthians 13.1—2.13, New Revised Standard Version of the Bible
1 May	Dorothy Day, *From Union Square to Rome*
2 May	Salah Abd al-Sabur, Egyptian Muslim poet
3 May	Mary Grey, *The Outrageous Pursuit of Hope*, Darton, Longman, and Todd, quoted with permission
4 May	Eric James, *Judge Not*, Christian Action, 1989, quoted with permission
5 May	From the Introduction to *Sweet and Sour*, Bengali Women's Support Group, South Yorkshire: apologies for incomplete reference
6 May	Mother Teresa of Calcutta: apologies for incomplete reference
7 May	Susan Griffin, *Made from this Earth*, Woman's Press, quoted with permission
8 May	Julian of Norwich, *Revelations of Divine Love*, translated by © Clifton Wolters, Penguin Classics, 1966, quoted with permission
9 May	Acharana Sutra, 3rd to 1st century BC
10 May	Gerard Hughes, *Walk to Jerusalem*, Darton, Longman, and Todd, quoted with permission
11 May	'Letter of the People of the Third World' signed by eighteen Roman Catholic bishops
12 May	Colin Morris, *Include Me Out*, Hodder and Stoughton, quoted with permission of William Neill-Hall Ltd
13 May	Humberto Lizardi, 'The poor and the rich', quoted by Dorothee Sölle, *Celebrating Resistance*, Mowbray, Continuum
14 May	Kahlil Gibran, Lebanese poet
15 May	Archbishop Joachim Ruhana of Burundi, assassinated 8 September 1996
16 May	Ignazio Silone: apologies for incomplete reference
17 May	Gerard Hughes, *Show me your Face*, Pax Christi, quoted with permission
18 May	Peter Maurin, co-founder of the Catholic Worker Movement
19 May	On St Brigid of Kildare, adapted from 'The Lives of the Saints' from *The Book of Lismore*
20 May	Quoted by Hyun Kyung Chung, *Voices of Women: An Asian Anthology*, Orbis Books, reprinted in *Struggle to be the Sun Again*, SCM Press, quoted with permission

21 May	John Dominic Crossan, *The Birth of Christianity*, Harper San Francisco, 1998, quoted with permission
22 May	Henri Nouwen, *Our Greatest Gift*, Hodder and Stoughton, quoted with permission
23 May	Edith Sitwell, 'The Song of the Cold', *Collected Poems*, David Higham Associates, quoted with permission
24 May	John Wesley: apologies for incomplete reference
25 May	Dorothy Day, *House of Hospitality*, Sheed and Ward, quoted with permission
26 May	Hasidic saying
27 May	Oscar Wilde, *An Ideal Husband*, Methuen
28 May	Edwina Gateley, *I Hear a Seed Growing*, Source Books, quoted with permission
29 May	Joan Robertson: apologies for incomplete reference
30 May	First Letter of John 3.7, New Revised Standard Version of the Bible
31 May	Blessing at the end of a Mass, source not traced
1 June	G. A. Studdert Kennedy: apologies for incomplete reference
2 June	Tales of the Hasidim
3 June	Julian of Norwich, *Revelations of Divine Love*, op. cit., quoted with permission
4 June	St Cyprian of Carthage: apologies for incomplete reference
5 June	Kahlil Gibran, Lebanese poet: apologies for incomplete reference
6 June	Dom Helder Camara, Archbishop of Recife: apologies for incomplete reference
7 June	Father Daniel Berrigan, SJ: apologies for incomplete reference
8 June	Evaristo, Cardinal Aris of Sao Paulo, *AIDS – Challenge for our Church*
9 June	From Robert Ehlberg's Introduction to Dorothy Day, *Selected Writings*
10 June	Dorothee Sölle, *Celebrating Resistance*, Mowbray, Continuum
11 June	Ralph Waldo Emerson: apologies for incomplete reference
12 June	Hallam Tennyson, *The Haunted Mind*, André Deutsch
13 June	Louis Evely: apologies for incomplete reference
14 June	Dorothy Day, *The Insulted and the Injured*, 1955 quoted with permission of Marquette University Libraries
15 June	Mohammed the Prophet: apologies for incomplete reference
16 June	Father Flor McCarthy, *Windows on the Gospel*, Dominican Publications
17 June	Yergeny Yevtushenko, *A Precocious Autobiography*, 1967, Harvill Press, quoted with permission
18 June	Dorothy Day, from *The Catholic Worker*, 1940, quoted with permission of Marquette University Libraries
19 June	Father Ronald Rolheiser, From an article in *The Catholic Herald*, 1993, quoted with permission

20 June   Bishop Richard Holloway, permission given personally
21 June   Sheila Cassidy, permission given personally
22 June   Mother Teresa of Calcutta: apologies for incomplete reference
23 June   Mary Grey: apologies for incomplete reference
24 June   Feast of St John the Baptist. Gospel according to St Luke
               3.10–14, New Revised Standard Version of the Bible
25 June   Leslie Griffiths, *Seasons of Life*, Methodist Publishing House,
               1996
26 June   Vinoba Bhave, *Moved by Love*, Green Books Ltd 1994, quoted
               with permission
27 June   William Wordsworth: apologies for incomplete reference
28 June   John Wesley: apologies for incomplete reference
29 June   Feast of St Peter and St Paul. The Letter to the Ephesians
               2.19, New Revised Standard Version of the Bible
30 June   Anonymous

1 July   Geiko Muller-Fahrenholz, *The Art of Forgiveness*, Council of
               Churches of Britain and Ireland
2 July   Elizabeth Jennings, *Moments of Grace*, Carcanet Press, quoted
               with permission
3 July   Feast of St Thomas. Edward Shillitoe, *Jesus of the Scars and
               Other Poems*
4 July   Martin Luther King Jnr, *Strength to Love*, Fontana, 1969,
               Hodder and Stoughton, also US 1963, renewed 1991, copy-
               right Coretta Scott King and the heirs to the estate, quoted
               with permission
5 July   Martin Luther King Jnr, op. cit., quoted with permission
6 July   Carlo Caretto, *In Search of Beyond*, Darton, Longman, and
               Todd, quoted with permission
7 July   Ann Bird, *Made to Care*, Methodist Publishing House
8 July   Algernon Charles Swinburne, 'Ave atque Vale'
9 July   C. S. Lewis, *The Business of Heaven*, Fount
10 July   Olivier Clément, *The Roots of Christian Mysticism*, New City,
               quoted with permission
11 July   Hannah Arendt, *The Human Condition*, University of Chicago
               Press, quoted with permission
12 July   Naim Ateek, *Justice and only Justice: A Palestinian Theology of
               Liberation*, Orbis Books, quoted with permission
13 July   Donald Nicholl, *The Testing of Hearts*, Darton, Longman, and
               Todd, quoted with permission
14 July   Sybil Phoenix, quoted by Brian Frost, *Women and Forgiveness*,
               Fount, 1988, quoted by permission of Sybil Phoenix
15 July   Philip Potter, *Life in all its Fulness*, World Council of Churches
16 July   Memorial on the east wall of the chapel at New College,
               Oxford, remembering the German undergraduates who
               fought in the First World War
17 July   The Buddha, Vimalakirtinirdesha Sutra 5

18 July	Oscar Wilde, 'The Ballad of Reading Gaol'
19 July	Elias Chacour, *Blood Brothers*, Chosen Books, quoted with permission
20 July	Gwen Cashmore and Joan Puls, *Clearing the Way*, World Council of Churches
21 July	Denis Tuohy, From an article in *The Tablet*, 21 February 1998, quoted with permission
22 July	*Sayings of the Desert Fathers*: apologies for incomplete reference
23 July	Corrie Ten Boom, *The Hiding Place*, Hodder and Stoughton, quoted with permission
24 July	Rabbi Hugo Gryn in an interview on BBC Radio 4 in 1987
25 July	Donald Nicholl, John Todd Memorial Lecture, 1994
26 July	Geiko Muller-Fahrenholz, op. cit. 1 July
27 July	Christian de Cherge, prior of a monastery in Algeria, in a letter written shortly before he was assassinated in May 1996
28 July	Michael Lapsley in an interview on BBC Radio 4 in 1995
29 July	Frances Lawrence, Letter to George's School in Maida Vale, London following the murder of its headmaster, quoted with personally given permission
30 July	Peter Storey, From on article 'A Different Kind of Justice' in *The Christian Century*
31 July	Brian Frost, *Struggling to Forgive*, HarperCollins, 1998, quoted with permission
1 August	Sister Stanislaus Kennedy, op. cit. 3 January
2 August	Martin Luther King, shortly before his assassination, 1963, copyright renewed 1991, Coretta Scott King, quoted with permission
3 August	Rabbi Albert Friedlander: apologies for incomplete reference
4 August	Peter Windram, writing in *The Tablet*, quoted by permission
5 August	Joan Chittister, *In Search of Belief*, Liguori/Triumph, 1999, and Crossroad Publishing, quoted by permission
6 August	The Feast of the Transfiguration. Desmond Tutu, From the Foreword to Brian Frost, *The Politics of Peace*, Darton, Longman, and Todd, quoted by permission
7 August	John Orens, 'Vision and Paradox', in ed. Kenneth Leech, *Conrad Noel and the Catholic Crusade*, Jubilee Group, 1993, quoted with permission
8 August	Richard Holloway, *Stranger in the Wings*, SPCK, quoted with personally given permission
9 August	Nelson Mandela, Inaugural Speech as President of South Africa, 1994
10 August	Kenneth Leech, *The Eye of the Storm*, Darton, Longman, and Todd, quoted by permission
11 August	Austin Smith, *Journeying with God*, Sheed and Ward, quoted by permission

12 August	J. H. Oldham, quoted in Clements, *Faith on the Frontier*, T. & T. Clark, quoted by permission
13 August	Desmond Tutu, quoted by permission
14 August	Jon Snow in an interview with Andrew Davidson in *The Independent* on Sunday, April 1995
15 August	The Feast of the Assumption of the Blessed Virgin Mary. John Newton, *Heart Speaks to Heart*, Darton, Longman, and Todd, quoted by permission
16 August	Henry Edward, Cardinal Manning, quoted in a source not traced
17 August	Father Robert Murray, *The Cosmic Covenant*, Sheed and Ward, quoted by permission
18 August	Barbara Ward: apologies for incomplete reference
19 August	Mark Santer in a sermon at his installation as Bishop Birmingham, 3 October 1987, quoted by permission
20 August	Thomas Bewick/H. U. Reay, in an article in *The Friend*
21 August	George Eliot, *Middlemarch*
22 August	Swami Paranahatsu Ysgananda
23 August	St Hilda
24 August	Trevor Huddleston, *Naught for your Comfort*, Collins, 1953, p.16
25 August	Dalit song quoted by David Haslam, *Caste Out!*, Churches Together in Britain and Ireland
26 August	Aimé Cesare, African poet: apologies for incomplete reference
27 August	Catherine Shelley, quoted in *Journey to the Millennium*, NBCW
28 August	The Talmud
29 August	Thomas Merton: apologies for incomplete reference
30 August	Michael Lapsley, quoted in *Priest and Partisan*, Ocean Press
31 August	Christopher Fry, *A Sleep of Prisoners*, OUP, 1951, quoted with permission of Christopher Fry
1 September	Father Diarmuid O'Laoghaire SJ, *Mary in Irish Spirituality*, Gill
2 September	Dorothy Day, *House of Hospitality*
3 September	Source unknown
4 September	Monica Furlong, *A Dangerous Delight*, SPCK
5 September	Father Bede Griffiths, quoted by Andrew Harvey and Mark Matousek, *Dialogues with a Modern Mystic*, Theosophical Publishing House
6 September	Peter Daino, *Mary, Mother of Sorrows, Mother of Defiance*, Orbis Books, quoted by permission
7 September	Herbert O'Driscoll, *Portrait of a Woman*, Seabury Press
8 September	Feast of the Blessed Virgin Mary. Gaelic prayer: apologies for incomplete reference
9 September	Herbert O'Driscoll, op. cit. 7 September
10 September	Dante Alighieri: apologies for incomplete reference
11 September	Ivone Gabara, From an article in *The Month*
12 September	Gordon Wakefield, *Mary's Place in Christian Dialogue*, St Paul Publications, quoted by permission

13 September   Oscar Wilde, 'San Miniato'

14 September   Padraic Pearse, 'Prayer to Mary', written for his mother before his execution, 1916

15 September   Kathy Galloway, *Love Burning Deep*, SPCK

16 September   Maria de Medici, Queen of France, d. 1642 'To the Virgin'

17 September   Ivone Gebara, op. cit. 11 September

18 September   Morris West, From an article in *The Catholic Herald*, December 1992, quoted with permission

19 September   Anonymous

20 September   Dorothy Sayers, *The Human Not Quite Human*, quoted with permission of David Higham Associates

21 September   Father Frei Betto, OP: apologies for incomplete reference

22 September   Gandhi the Mahatma: apologies for incomplete reference

23 September   Gandhi the Mahatma: apologies for incomplete reference

24 September   Oscar Romero, *The Violence of Love*, Plough Publishing House, quoted with permission

25 September   Hans Urs von Balthasar: apologies for incomplete reference

26 September   Thomas Merton: apologies for incomplete reference

27 September   Joseph Campbell, 'The Old Woman', Paterson Publications, 1949

28 September   Source untraced

29 September   The Feast of St Michael and All Angels. Guy Butler, from the poem 'Mercy', quoted in *A Book of Hope*

30 September   St Hildegaard of Bingen: apologies for incomplete reference

1 October   Thomas Merton, *The Asian Journal of Thomas Merton*, Sheldon Press

2 October   Sufi mystic

3 October   William Penn: apologies for incomplete reference

4 October   Rumi, Persian Sufi mystic

5 October   James Roose-Evans, *Inner Journey, Outer Journey*, Darton, Longman, and Todd, quoted by permission

6 October   Sister Catherine, *Poor in Spirit: Modern Parables*, Charles LePetit

7 October   Evelyn Underhill: apologies for incomplete reference

8 October   St Nicholas of Cusa: apologies for incomplete reference

9 October   Swami Iswar Prasad, a Roman Catholic monk, speaking at Anjali Ashram in 1991

10 October   John V. Taylor, *The Go-Between God*, SCM Press, quoted by permission

11 October   S. Wesley Ariarajah, *Not without my Neighbour*, Churches Together in Britain and Ireland

12 October   Brother David Steindl-Rast OSB: apologies for incomplete reference

13 October   Ibn-al-Arabi, Persian Sufi mystic

14 October   John Prickett, *Godspells*, The Book Guild, quoted by permission

15 October   Sister Stanislaus Kennedy, op. cit. 3 January

16 October   Dorothy Day, 'Room for Christ', *The Catholic Worker*, 1945,
               quoted with permission
17 October .   Machthild of Magdeburg, quoted by Lucy Menzies, *Mirror of
               the Holy*, Mowbray
18 October   Donald Nicholl, from an article in the magazine *Inter-Faith*
19 October   Charles Elliott, *Praying the Kingdom*, Darton, Longman, and
               Todd, quoted by permission
20 October   Evelyn Underhill, from a letter to a friend
21 October   Desmond Tutu, from an interview in *The Independent*, 1994
22 October   William Temple: apologies for incomplete reference
23 October   Jurgen Moltmann, *The Source of Life*, SCM Press, quoted by
               permission
24 October   Brother Daniel Faivre, *Transcendence: Prayers of People of Faith*
25 October   From a prayer leaflet for racial justice published by Churches
               Together in Britain and Ireland
26 October   Colin Winter, when bishop-in-exile from Namibia
27 October   Brother Lawrence, *Oratory of the Heart*, quoted by permission
28 October   Ann Bird, op. cit. 7 July
29 October   Père Grou, 1731–1803
30 October   Jubilee prayer in St Michael's Parish, Liverpool, quoted in *The
               Tablet*, quoted by permission
31 October   R. S. Thomas, 'Folk Tale', *Experimenting with an Amen*,
               Macmillan

1 November   All Saints' Day. Martin Luther: apologies for incomplete
               reference
2 November   Derek Webster, *Our Time Now*, Kenelm Press
3 November   Christopher Fry, *Thor, with Angels*, 1946, quoted by kind
               permission of the author
4 November   Charlotte Mitchell, *I Want to go Home*, Souvenir Press, 1991,
               quoted with permission
5 November   Henri Nouwen, op. cit. 22 May
6 November   Brother Ramon SSF: apologies for incomplete reference
7 November   Metropolitan Anthony of Sourozh, quoted in *Seasons of the
               Spirit*, SPCK
8 November   Emily Dickinson: apologies for incomplete reference
9 November   Victor Hugo, 1880: apologies for incomplete reference
10 November   Margaret Stansgate, *My Exit Visa*, Hutchinson, 1992
11 November   Armistice Day 1918. Siegfried Sassoon, 'Reconciliation', *The
               War Poems*, Faber & Faber, quoted with kind permission of
               George Sassoon
12 November   Louie Horne, 'Mourn us not', Quaker friend of Nadir
               Dinshaw by correspondence
13 November   Count Helmut von Moltke writing to his wife on the eve of his
               execution, quoted in *A German of the Resistance, The Last Letters
               of Count Helmut James von Moltke*, OUP, 1947, quoted with
               permission

14 November   John Harriott, *The Empire of the Heart*, Templegate Publishers, 1990

15 November   William Penn: apologies for incomplete reference

16 November   Rabindranath Tagore, *Gitanji*, Brandon Publishing, Boston, 1942, quoted by permission

17 November   Ravidas, 17th century Hindu poet

18 November   President Jefferson to John Adams at the end of their lives

19 November   Father Flor McCarthy SDB, *Funeral Liturgies*

20 November   John Greenleaf Whittier: apologies for incomplete reference

21 November   Aaron Gallegos and Rose Marie Berger, in the magazine *Sojourners*, July 1993

22 November   Gerald O'Collins, from an article in *The Tablet*, 1 January 2000, quoted by permission

23 November   Toni Morrison, *Sula*, Chatto and Windus, 1973, quoted by permission

24 November   Oliver Gogarty, 'Non Dolet'

25 November   Donald Nicholl, from an article 'My Last Voyage' in The Tablet, 1997, quoted by permission

26 November   Felicity Arbuthnot: apologies for incomplete reference

27 November   Father Donal O'Doherty, *Experiences in a City Parish*

28 November   Rabindranath Tagore, op. cit. 14 November

29 November   Julia Esquivel, 'I am not afraid of death', *Threatened with Resurrection*, Brethren Press, 1982, quoted by permission

30 November   Annie Dillard, *Pilgrim at Tinker Creek*, Harpers Magazine Press, 1974

1 December   Donagh O'Shea, *I Remember your Name in the Night*, Dominican Publications

2 December   Jurgen Moltmann, op. cit. 23 October

3 December   Ann Wroe, from an article in *The Tablet*, 18 December 1999, quoted by permission

4 December   John Meade Falkner, 'Christmas Joy: The Family Sitting', apologies for incomplete reference

5 December   Rowan Williams, 'Advent Calendar', op. cit. 1 March

6 December   John A. T. Robinson: apologies for incomplete reference

7 December   Søren Kierkegaard: apologies for incomplete reference

8 December   Hannah Whitall Pearsall Smith, *A Religious Rebel*, Nisbet, 1949, quoted by permission

9 December   Gerard Hughes: apologies for incomplete reference

10 December   Brother Lawrence: apologies for incomplete reference

11 December   Jean Pierre de Caussade: apologies for incomplete reference

12 December   Joan Chittister, *The Rule of Benedict: Insights for the Ages*, Crossroad Publishing, 1992

13 December   Mario Marazziti: apologies for incomplete reference

14 December   Thomas Merton: apologies for incomplete reference

15 December   Donald Nicholl, *The Beatitude of Truth*, Darton, Longman, and Todd, quoted by permission

16 December	Dag Hammarskjøld, *Markings*, Faber & Faber
17 December	The Notebooks of Florence Allshorn
18 December	Dom Helder Camara, Archbishop of Recife: apologies for incomplete reference
19 December	Paul Weller: apologies for incomplete reference
20 December	Musimbi Kanyoro, *Your Story is My Story, My Story is Your Story*, World Council of Churches, 1999
21 December	Elizabeth Jennings, 'Mary's Part', from *The Tablet* for 21 December, 1991
22 December	Bishop Michael Hare Duke, 'Christmas in the Philippines', from a Christmas letter to family and friends
23 December	Peter Millar, *The Iona Community*, SCM Canterbury Press, 1997, quoted by permission
24 December	U. A. Fanthorpe, 'BC AD', *Selected Poems*, Penguin, 1986, rights with Harry Chambers
25 December	The Gospel according to John 1.14
26 December	Lucille Clifton: apologies for incomplete reference
27 December	David Blanchflower: apologies for incomplete reference
28 December	Excerpt from an Arabic Gospel
29 December	op. cit. 28 December
30 December	Reuben Alves, *Tomorrow's Child*, SCM Press, quoted by permission
31 December	St John Chrysostom, 'On Providence'